Friend of the Soul

Friend of the Soul

A Benedictine Spirituality of Work

Norvene Vest

COWLEY PUBLICATIONS

Cambridge ◆ Boston
Massachusetts

Published in the United States of America by Cowley Publications, a division
of the Society of St. John the Evangelist. No portion of this book may be
reproduced, stored in or introduced into a retrieval system, or transmitted,
in any form or by any means—including photocopying—without the prior
written permission of Cowley Publications, except in the case of brief
quotations embodied in critical articles and reviews.

Library of Congress Cataloging-in-Publication Data:
Vest, Norvene.
    Friend of the soul: a Benedictine spirituality of work / Norvene Vest.
        p.   cm.
    Includes bibliographical references.
    ISBN 1-56101-138-X (pbk.)
    1. Work—Religious aspects—Catholic Church. 2. Benedictines—
Spiritual life. 3. Benedict, Saint, Abbot of Monte Cassino. Regula. I. Title.
    BX1795.W67V47   1996
    248.8'8—dc20   96-35855
                                                                        CIP

The translation of the Rule of St. Benedict quoted throughout is by Fr. Luke
Dysinger, OSB, and published in Norvene Vest's *Preferring Christ* (Trabuco
Canyon, Calif.: Source Books, 1991). Used by permission.

Scripture quotations are taken from the *New Revised Standard Version* of
the Bible, © by the Division of Christian Education of the National Council
of the Churches of Christ in the USA. Used by permission. All rights reserved.

Cynthia Shattuck, editor; Vicki Black, copyeditor and designer

This book is printed on acid-free paper and was produced in Canada.

Cowley Publications • 28 Temple Place • Boston, Massachusetts 02111
1-800-225-1534 • http://www.cowley.org/~cowley

This book is dedicated to the group of people who meet monthly in our living room to share how Benedictine spirituality forms our lives. We call ourselves a "Benedictine cell"—cell meaning a nucleus or living center, a small and prayerful place connected to a larger unit, which in our case is St. Andrew's Benedictine Abbey in Valyermo. These friends have supported me through the months of gestation of this book, often suggesting ideas, but more often freely giving that warm acceptance and generous prayer in which my soul is befriended and my work emerges.

I am especially appreciative of the sturdy and bracing support of Cowley's director, Cynthia Shattuck, whose vocation, stewardship, and obedience are a vivid reminder that holy work is alive and well in our midst.

Contents

Introduction

Work as a Holy Task

Work is the friend of the soul.
(RB 48:1, rephrased)

Can you envision your work as a holy task? The purpose of this book is to offer some ways of doing just that by drawing on the wisdom of the Rule of St. Benedict, a way of life developed for ordinary people living in communities as monks and nuns, dedicated to prayer, work, and the worship of God. Possibly you have already glanced at some books whose titles include the words "work" and "monastic" and have been somewhat disappointed to find a discussion of Benedictine life as a whole yet little attention paid to work as an essential part of life. This lack is particularly frustrating for those of us who are struggling to discover *how* work can become more integrated into our life and faith outside a cloister. Too often the ways we earn our living seem almost hostile to faith, interested only in fragments of our whole selves and requiring that we leave our capacities to envision and to embrace at home.

Yet the Benedictine perspective continues to puzzle and even tantalize us as we try to see our "worldly work" as sacred. We sense that the Benedictines have something that we are missing. Maybe that "something" only means that they live together in intentional community, supported by a regular rhythm of prayer—yet their life also seems to teach them something particular about work itself. Surely we can learn from them, applying their "secret" to our own settings, along with such rhythms of prayer and community as are possible for men and women who are fully engaged with families, study, and earning a living.

Monastic work can never be separated from prayer. Indeed, the informal motto of Benedictine life has long been known as *ora et labora*, prayer and work. The motto is not work *is* prayer, but rather prayer *and* work! The most important of these three words is *and*: there must be a balance of prayer and activity in a full human life. The rhythms of silence, common prayer, and holy reading discussed in my earlier book, *No Moment Too Small*, are understood to be necessary foundations for this exploration of monastic work. Prayer punctuates and penetrates Benedictine work at every point; work poses questions of prayer that give it urgency. We may imagine cloistered religious are free from the pressures of the world of work, yet the Rule itself envisions nothing less than the integration of the whole life of the Christian in the service of God. This very unity of work and prayer gives Benedictines a particular orientation toward work, infusing their work with the quality of holiness we are seeking in our own lives.

Behind the Rule lies Benedict's understanding of the purpose and quality of human life. Why are we created at all? What is the optimum relationship between human beings and the created world, and between human beings and God? Are we meant to experience our work and our life as problem, punishment, or unfolding gift? What does scripture have to say? In the first chapter of Genesis we see God at work creating the universe and finding pleasure in it. Then God creates a being sharing the divine image and likeness, male and female, whom God blesses and gives dominion over every living thing.

God calls all things good. Then, resting from the work, God hallows a day of rest for all creation too (2:1-4).

This story of creation told in the first chapter of Genesis conveys a sense of harmony and right relation among all: God, human beings, and other creatures. Blessing is conveyed throughout the story, as well as God's delight in goodness. In this view, human labor is modeled on God's labor, fruitful activity that flows forth from the essence of one's being, as well as in beneficial care for others. Our work here on earth is "co-creative," which means it is shared with the living God. God's original intention was that work express the unique gifts and qualities of each person in the service of a unified whole, like a melody that is diminished by the absence of any single note. Many of us harbor some form of this vision: a deep, often unspoken sense that we have been created for a special purpose, that we have a serious and holy calling to be expressed through active engagement with the world around us—that is, through our work.

The New Testament reiterates these themes, reminding us that as baptized persons we are members of the body of Christ in the world and through us Christ's work in the world is ongoing. Thus Paul wrote in his letter to the Romans, "We have been buried with Christ Jesus by baptism into death, so that, just as Christ was raised from the dead by the glory of the Father, so we too might walk in newness of life" (Rom. 6:4), and to the church at Corinth, "If anyone is in Christ, there is a new creation....All this is from God, who reconciled us to himself through Christ, and has given us the ministry of reconciliation" (2 Cor. 5:17-18). These are bold assertions about what the life of every baptized person is meant to be, walking in newness of life and continuing Christ's ministry of reconciliation. The "work" of the reconciliation of the world to God and of the transformation of all things into their intended fullness in Christ is in part *our* work, no less than God's. Each one of us has an essential role to play in the divine plan; for this we were born. Remote as this may sound from the labors we undertake each day, a longing for this reality is placed within the human heart, leaving us restless and unsatisfied until we begin to live in fidelity to it.

Accordingly, we hold a vision of human work not only as a means to support ourselves and our families and as a genuine means of charity and service to others, but also as an expression of our particular gifts as partners with God in bringing the whole of creation to its intended fulfillment.[1] Human work is meant to be a holy endeavor. In his Rule St. Benedict reminds the monks that work is the friend of the soul itself (RB 48:1, paraphrased), one of the means by which we love and serve God instead of something separate and accidental to our faith. Benedict urges further that all monastics work on behalf of one another, "for in this way greater reward is obtained and love is acquired" (RB 35:2).

Work is meant to be a holy endeavor. Such a vision forms the context for our own daydreams about what we might contribute to our own and one another's work so that it can be more fulfilling for ourselves and more beneficial to others. This vision insists that our work matters, not simply as a means to make money, but as an expression of faith and being.

In the following chapters we will carefully unfold Benedict's Rule to learn how it embodies this vision of human life and work. Although an important theological engagement with ordinary work as holy human endeavor occurred at the time of the Reformation, with Luther's valuing of human labor as the way ordinary Christians lived out their sacred calling, centuries of Christian experience and reflection on work preceded that time. In the pivotal synthesis of Christian ideas brought together in the sixth century in Benedict's Rule we find a gentle but firm, life-enhancing, and spirit-filled understanding of the value of human labor. In an age when most physical work was delegated to slaves and barbarians, Benedict treated the human body and human work as fundamental ingredients of the holy life. In his view labor was not only dignified, but conducive to holiness. Prayer was more likely to take root in our lives when anchored in practical work.

The mystical element in Benedictine work includes a way of seeing, a contemplative attitude facilitated by a practice of awareness and reflection on God's presence revealed in every encounter. Work requires reverence in touching and handling material things, for "all tools and goods are to be regarded as though they were the consecrated vessels of the altar" (RB 31:10). Work punctuated by prayer enables both to become vehicles for the natural emergence of deep insights about God. In the Rule Benedict emphasized the essentially sacred nature of human work, and the practical context of his advice yields helpful guidance for our specific situations, too.

In my own work of lecturing and teaching I often hear people speak of a sense of helplessness about their work. Complex issues are raised, heated exchanges occur, and what emerges is the fact that many Christians believe the numbing complexity of modern work to be so deeply entrenched in our society that it is beyond the reach of the gospel of Christ. How could Jesus—much less Benedict—understand the difficult dilemmas they face in their work? They feel stuck, certain that traditional faith cannot help them because it is rooted in a simpler time and place utterly remote from the pain and tension of contemporary work. Perhaps this resistance is due to the fact that many of us have unwittingly adopted the cynical and despairing attitudes prevalent around us. We see the world as so broken and wounded that it is impossible to do the right thing; if we do take a stand, we will be left out on a limb looking like fools, with nothing to show for it. We don't believe that God is here with us, holding out possibilities we can actually choose, and so we have forgotten how to take risks, to make commitments and support one another in doing so.

Benedict's Rule illumines three basic principles about work enfolded in the context of prayer:

(1) vocation, being called to what we do;

(2) stewardship, taking care of what is given; and

(3) obedience, serving one another.

These themes will be developed in the following chapters as we look at modern expectations and experiences of work and then explore language and examples in the Rule of St. Benedict that reveal the meaning of these rich theological ideas for human work. Throughout I will suggest ways of applying these principles to contemporary work, as a means of gaining a surer sense of the sacredness of the work we do.

Although I hope to illuminate Benedict's vision of sacred work and to help create openings for that vision in our own lives, I have no illusions that his vision is easy to implement. On the contrary, it is extremely challenging and difficult to apply to one's own work the relatively simple Benedictine principles I will unfold. Therefore I strongly recommend that you find several others with whom to read this book and take your time exploring with one another the possibilities suggested in each chapter. Each chapter ends with a list of reflection exercises, which will help to focus on your immediate situation and the next best step, rather than on some point in the future. Being part of a prayer or support group can help each person be realistic as well as inspired, so that choices can be effective—if not for the situation, at least for the choice-maker. Remember that the Holy Spirit is in your midst, helping you.

Benedict summarizes his invitation to this way of life with these words:

We have, therefore, to establish a school of the Lord's service. In the institution of it, we hope to establish nothing that is harsh or burdensome. But if anything is somewhat strictly laid down, according to the dictates of equity and for the amendment of vices, or for the preservation of love, do not therefore flee in dismay from the way of salvation, which cannot be other than narrow at the beginning. (RB Prologue 45-48)

In our work, may we be graced to find the narrow way neither too harsh nor too burdensome, so that we may persevere toward love.

One

In Times Like These

The World of St. Benedict

Be learned in the law of God, that [you] may
know how to bring forth new things and old.
(RB 64:9)

Benedict is an important source of guidance for us about work. Although distant in time, his own age was filled with difficulties Christians face in any age, and he reflected on scripture with many of the same questions our hearts hold. Benedict always asks, "What does it mean to live according to the gospel *in times like these?*" Behind our doubt and cynicism about our work and the complex world in which we live, isn't that also our fundamental question? How can we be faithful to the call of Christ in this troubling moment in history? How do we find God in the midst of a chaotic and distraught world?

It may help us to see Benedict's Rule as relevant to our work if we have a better understanding of the world in which Benedict lived. Benedict and his twin sister Scholastica were born in the last decades of the fifth century in a rural area north of Rome. Only seventy years earlier the barbarian invader

Alaric and his armies had conquered Rome itself and ushered in a time of tremendous social dislocation, upheaval, and change. From the beginning of the third century the *pax Romana* had so unified the Roman Empire that all the different parts of the known world had flourished within one economic system marked by free trade and increasing prosperity, but now the economy was fluctuating wildly.

Each geographic area had a specialty according to its natural resources, and the excellent roads and sea routes still made easy exchanges possible. Cloth, wine, corn, furs, lead, cheese, and oil were readily bought and sold among Egypt, Cappadocia, Spain, Greece, Gaul, and Britain. The region where Benedict and Scholastica were born, the Sabine country in Italy, is set within the mountain ranges of the Apennines, with a fertile valley floor populated by sturdy and grave farmers. Their fine cheeses would have been carted out to the nearby Flaminian Way and thence to Rome, and long wood timbers would have been transported the short distance over land to the Adriatic Sea to be used in boat construction.

While the Sabines pursued a fairly simple way of life even during the prosperous years of the Roman Empire, other regions were avid consumers of foreign delicacies, and imports to Rome had exceeded exports for several centuries. Benedict's grandmother might have proudly displayed a matched pair of glass goblets acquired by her husband in Egypt during more prosperous times. Although the Roman silver, gold, and copper mines were gradually depleted and the new coinage was insufficient to support such exotic tastes, people did not relinquish their habits willingly and inflation became a serious problem. Though government income was declining, military costs remained high as Rome sought to contain inherent tensions among the many cultures of the far-flung empire.

Enterprising local tradesmen charged exorbitant prices to their government-backed clients, the Roman soldiers. Evening conversation in Benedict's household might have turned to economics—the copper coin did not buy as much as it used to—and then drifted to the recent ruckus that broke out when the local owner of the baths began charging Roman soldiers double the local price. Several drunken soldiers had angrily lashed out at the owner and cut off his ear with a sword, and each party had brought charges against the other to the local town senate.

Benedict's father, as a member of the provincial gentry, would have been greatly preoccupied with delivering a fair judgment. The town senate was bound by the decree of the previous century by the emperor Diocletian establishing maximum price levels throughout the empire and threatening capital punishment for the "evil greed" that fed inflation. Benedict's father strongly condemned greed, but he also knew that the current economy made it very difficult for honest tradesmen to make ends meet and his own trading often took the form of goods and services instead of cash. While not condoning the civil violence of the soldiers, Benedict's father could see that they resented being overcharged, even though the government did reimburse their normal expenses.

The town senate was the official local arm of the imperial government, and the *curia*, or senators, were personally responsible for payment of taxes to the central Roman authorities. If bad harvests made it impossible for the small farmers to pay their taxes, the *curia* were nonetheless required to pay the central government the full amount. Such laws invited corruption, as *curiales* found ways to avoid the personal ruin entailed by full payment of taxes.

Scholastica might have confided to Benedict that she overheard the visiting stranger from Rome ask their father to give him a list of names of his colleagues who were cheating on their taxes. What would happen to him if he refused? What is the best relationship between the rights of the individual and the needs of the many? Does an individual's style of life have a direct connection with the practice of virtue? Are beauty and luxury the same thing? What happens when secrecy and dishonesty flourish? Is grumbling a helpful release of frustration, or a negative brake on healthy solutions? Benedict would have stored such questions away for further thought.

A Blending of Cultures

A tremendous migration of northern barbarian tribes into Italy in a search for home and soil also took place in the fourth and fifth centuries. The northern peoples called it the *Volkwanderung,* the wandering of the folk; the Romans called it an invasion. The incoming tribes were chiefly Germanic peoples—Ostrogoths, Vandals, Franks—who were primitive compared with sophisticated Romans. Agrarian and largely illiterate, vigorous and impulsive, they were chiefly linked through unwritten laws based on blood ties. Yet they admired the achievements of Rome and sought to learn Latin, shored up municipal buildings and public works, and strengthened legal customs.

Thus in Benedict's time a Germanic society was gradually settling down upon Roman foundations, with all the chaos attendant upon two radically different cultures merging. Relative peace was achieved during the thirty-three year "reign," ending in 526, of the "emperor" Theodoric, an Ostrogoth king who as a child had been kidnapped and taken to Constantinople but now had the blessing of the eastern emperor to rule Italy. Theodoric's dream was *civilitas,* a word used often by his Roman secretary, Cassiodorus, to express the union of virile force and polished culture he envisioned for his kingdom.

Rural areas like the Sabine home of Benedict and Scholastica were particularly affected by the influx of new peoples into Italy. Even when Rome defeated the invaders and sought to press them into service as agricultural workers, it was quickly discovered that Ostrogothic tribesmen made obstinate and volatile slaves; the land was better cultivated if the newcomers were set up on small plots as independent farmers. So Benedict and Scholastica's neighbors were German tenants as well as small Italian landholders; Ostrogoths even became imperial office-holders and local officials. Intermarriage was still legally forbidden, but a practical working relationship developed as Italians and Germans lived and worked side by side.

Benedict would no doubt have absorbed all these differing cultures. His own town of Nursia was walled, but less to keep out "foreigners" than to emphasize its role as the market center where both Gothic and Italian farmers brought their goods. Benedict and Scholastica loved the noisy, multilingual market days, and always sought out one stall in particular where blond and wild-haired Frederik would embrace them and whirl them up onto the back of his huge but now aging warhorse. One day Frederik confided to them that the old horse was glad no longer to be always on the move, but willingly gave up the turmoil of battle for the milder task of carting the heavy produce wagon back and forth into town.

New groups of land-hungry Goths continued to wander into Italy, and regular skirmishes occurred between small bands of armed men while desperate, homeless, and hungry people wandered everywhere. Settled farmers, no less than the townspeople, lived in constant fear of unexpected violence and they turned increasingly to large rural estate owners for protection. Many of these rural estates had inward-facing villas, or estate compounds, which combined the luxury of mosaic floors indoors with the practicality of fortlike defenses on the outer walls, behind which the household and neighbors could take refuge and defend themselves when necessary.

More than once Benedict's family fled for safety to a wealthy villa in their region. Sometimes assaults by warring bands were frightening and dangerous; more often, as soon as they saw they were outmaneuvered, the horsemen would ride away. While the families were gathered, the local lord encouraged exchange of information about problems and mutual support in common projects. In the Sabine region, as elsewhere, the town senate and its responsibilities to faraway Rome dwindled in importance compared to the growing sense of community in this "village" of people associated with the *potentiore*, or rural estate owner. A rough-and-ready economic and political alliance of neighbors gradually developed into a sense of mutual regard and support, with less dependence upon imported delicacies and more reliance upon what could be repaired or invented. Practical Italians like Benedict's father appreciated the experimental approach to problems contributed by the immigrant tribesmen. Women borrowed ideas freely from one another for the solution of common household problems. In the countryside, Theodoric's dream of *civilitas* began to come true in practical ways.

Benedict might well have a vivid memory of the first time all the nearby families gathered in a public assembly to discuss and resolve matters of common concern. It would have been a noisy, rowdy gathering, with the German families shouting out their approval and disapproval, but everyone would have left feeling that they had come to an agreement all could honor. Again, this would have given Benedict food for thought. Although it was troubling when people of differing viewpoints clashed, especially at first, the fruit of such chaos was often a new solution that benefited everyone. Initial prejudice between people strange to each other could be alleviated by coming together over common needs. Benedict observed how God could work constructively, even in the apparent antagonism of tradition and rapid change.[1]

Education and the Church

If a poor economy and the constant influx of new peoples were two of the major influences on the early life of Benedict and Scholastica, the church was the third. The members of their family were devout Christians who could trace their ancestry to a martyred saint in the earliest years of Constantine's reign. They would have regularly attended services at the parish church and been active in congregational affairs. Scholastica seemed to live close to God from her earliest years, and soon the family accepted her desire not to marry but to adopt the life of a consecrated virgin. Living at home in austerity and semi-seclusion, she would have been relieved of many household duties and assigned a nurse-servant who shared her religious commitment as well as her spinning and weaving tasks.

Benedict would have been taught by a local *rhetor*, a teacher paid by the state. Since the public system of education was suffering from inadequate government funding, Benedict may well have received most of his earliest education from Roman priests and monks who traveled through the area and stayed with the family. His tutor would have also taught Scholastica how to read and write, so that she could study scripture and copy religious manuscripts. These visits were especially cherished by Benedict and Scholastica, who were avid to hear news of the churches in Jerusalem and Africa as well as the ideas emerging from the great councils of Nicea, Constantinople, and Chalcedon. Although at that age they may not have been able to follow all of the complexities of the theological implications of Arianism or the doctrine of the Incarnation, they would have struggled with the significance of the creeds for their own beliefs.

When he became an adolescent Benedict's family sent him to Rome for further education, which would have focused on grammar and rhetoric as the necessary preparation for polite society, as well as a position in the civil service. Emphasis was placed on form, grammar, and technical perfection in thought and literature, quite apart from the substance; mannered eloquence was the chief goal of rhetorical style. Benedict might well have been frustrated at the ability of his fellow students to speak so well about nothing at all, and dismayed at their sophisticated cynicism. It was not unusual for students in his apartment to carry home portions of statues stolen from public gardens and plazas, caring little about such niceties as ownership in a city of ruined masonry, blackened and roofless buildings, and scattered debris.

The Rome of Benedict's studies was still a busy and cosmopolitan city, offering every form of amusement and pleasure, from the violence of the gladiatorial games to gossip about the decadent rich. In Rome he must have come face-to-face with the commonplace evils of his time—children sold into slavery or prostitution by their families, nobles using public office to increase private wealth. The ideal of Roman society was a life of leisure, with slaves providing for every want; Benedict would have seen the litters of the rich go by covered in silks whose cost would have paid his teacher's annual salary, and he no doubt often wondered about the connections among scarcity, greed, and violence. Can anyone uphold and strengthen personal virtue in a time when virtue is widely ridiculed as folly? Does private integrity have any impact on the common life?

For Benedict there could be no compromise: he dropped his studies and went off in "learned ignorance" to seek solitude and prayer in God alone—yet apparently the city did not leave him. As Benedict continued in prayer many of the conflicts and temptations that he viewed as alien in Rome began to emerge from within himself. Much of the suffering he had seen became grist for his intercessory prayer. Perhaps he thought about his barbarian neighbors at home, and wondered why the glory of Rome was so important to them; how could it matter so much to them to learn about and sustain the older civilization? For three years Benedict was alone with his God.

Neither an intellectual nor a scholar, Benedict did not communicate his newfound wisdom by what he said but by what he did (and did not do). As classical culture continued its decay and collapse, he saw the signs of vibrant new life. He perceived the evil in human affairs, but also renewal and rebirth, and he never gave up on the possibilities for creativity and action. Early in the sixth century Benedict founded a religious community on the top of Monte Cassino, on the main road between Rome and Naples. At the base of the mountain lived his sister Scholastica in a community of women, and the brother and sister often consulted together on the problems of daily life in their communities as well as the vision of God these communities upheld. Up and down the road below Monte Cassino traveled the tribes and armies whose interactions marked the end of one age and the beginning of another. The daily life and the legacy of these twins in their communities became almost "a visible boundary where a dying and a new-born age touch one another."[2]

Questions for Today

The questions Benedict asked about life in his world are not unlike our own, and as we reflect on the outlines of Benedict's life and times we can observe some of the questions about work and human activity in the world that are crucial for our time as well. These questions have to do with the best way to live, which each of us must prayerfully answer for ourselves. Benedict chose not to stay in Rome and become a part of the existing power structure or to incite mass protests to gain the attention of those in power. Although he initially withdrew in solitude for a time of reflection and discernment, he later returned to life in community, and there he crafted an approach to living the gospel that has survived long beyond his own lifetime.

Although Benedict lived at the cusp of a major historical shift—the end of the classical age and the beginning of the medieval world—he would have lacked that clear perspective himself. Our future is also cloudy: we cannot say with certainty whether a new age is on its way, already begun, or nearly ending. It is seldom easy to discern which are the signs of life and growth, and which point to deterioration and decay; yet it is Benedict's insistence on asking "What does it mean to live according to the gospel in times like these?" that makes his insights so helpful to us now. In the midst of collapse and chaos, he was able to concentrate on the signs of life he *did* see, and to work to strengthen and support those signs of the Holy Spirit's presence in human activity. Benedict can reveal a way for us of focusing on the good, the true, and the beautiful, while his Rule teaches us too how to work in cooperation with the realm of God always breaking into human history.

Two

Vocation

Being Called

What could be sweeter to us than this voice of the
Lord inviting us? Behold in lovingkindness
the Lord shows us the way of life.
(RB Prologue 19-20)

Do you have a vocation? Nowadays we often think that
the term "vocation" is limited to ministers, priests, and
those who take religious vows. Or we pray for "vocations" for
our monasteries and parish churches, asking God to send
people willing to devote their lives to the service of the church
and its institutions. Even the phrase "ministry of the laity"
usually seems to mean church work—joining the altar guild or
teaching Sunday school. When we think of our primary work,
the work we do every day to support ourselves, most of us
would say no if asked whether we have a vocation.

The Latin root for vocation is *vocare* and it means "to call."
In its earliest meaning, the word vocation meant that a person
was *called* by God to his or her work. If my work is a vocation,
then I feel that God has called me to that work. I sense God's
call because I am attracted and drawn to this work, and feel

that I am gifted for the work itself. Probably I have a sense that nothing else can truly satisfy me, and I believe that I am able to serve others through what I do. Vocation is what Dorothy Sayers meant when she wrote, "Work is not primarily a thing one does to live, but the thing one lives to do. It is, or should be, the full expression of the worker's faculties, the thing in which he finds spiritual, mental, and bodily satisfaction."[1]

What is it that we "live to do"? For many of us, it is not our work. Rather, we might agree with Huckleberry Finn that work is something a body is obliged to do! Others of us who think that we *do* live to work see that fact as a burden: work is so all-consuming that it squeezes everything else out of life.

Vocation, or Christian calling, can be elusive. It is sometimes associated with the Calvinist notion that God calls people to a specific (and fixed) state in life, a belief that could be used as self-justification by those who have wealth and influence against those who do not. Alternatively, vocation has been understood as draining and exhausting labor in the service of those in need. Or, as noted above, we may associate the term exclusively with a calling to vowed, or religious life, suggesting that vocation means some sort of withdrawal from the world and its pleasures. How can we understand vocation as a helpful insight into our daily work?

In thinking about this question, consider the story of a woman I'll call Charlene, who works as program director with a nonprofit organization that aids the urban poor. She has always considered herself a religious person even though for many years she has not attended church. As her children begin to grow up, she realizes that she wants a Christian community for them and a place where she herself can worship on Sunday, so she joins one of the local congregations. Because of Charlene's intellectual gifts and emotional warmth, she finds that she is president of the congregational board within three years. Although she blossoms in the community setting, Charlene is both disturbed and excited to find she is enjoying her volunteer activities at church more than her job; the work itself is fine, but her boss is emotionally unstable, and lately she has less tolerance for his outbursts.

Next Charlene attends a couple of seminars for people who are wondering about ordination and talks with several other women pastors, finding that they seem to be juggling the roles of parent, spouse, and minister with no more difficulty than she is having already. But the longer she explores it, the less inviting ordination seems. She has never been much of a student, so the thought of all the classes she would have to take is daunting, and she still has a deep and serious commitment to her present work, in which she has already invested over ten years. It occurs to her that she is probably called to "minister" just where she is, and she does not need ordination for that.

So Charlene begins to wonder how she can make her daily work seem more like her ministry. How can she develop a stronger sense of God's involvement with her—not merely at church, but at her office as well? She discovers that she is going to work each day with a new curiosity and attention. Each morning she prays, "God, how will you meet me today?" and then she watches. One day as she hurries to the nearby fast-food restaurant, she bumps into an old man who asks her for money to eat. Doubtfully she gives him a dollar, only to observe that he does indeed order a hamburger. From her adjacent table, Charlene watches the old man eat in the slow and careful way that the very hungry do, and tears spring to her eyes. She only has time to finish half her sandwich, and she wonders if he would be offended if she offers him the other half. Hesitantly, she makes her offer, and the old man's eyes light up as he blesses her. When she returns to the office to find her boss in one of his rages, she hardly notices because the sense of blessing is so strong with her.

On another day Charlene makes a site visit to a teen center that welcomes members of all the local gangs, provided they put aside their rivalries while there. She watches several boys concentrate intensely on building a model airplane together, stunned by her sudden realization that these boys are just children yet some of them have probably murdered others. She is happy she had a part in funding such crucial experiments and grateful for the commitment of the adult directors who make it possible for kids to be kids, if only for a few hours a day. She cannot imagine devoting her life to anything else.

Before, she thought that ministry meant doing things for others, and while she is still trying to serve as wisely and well as she can, she knows it is her ministry that blesses her. She is privileged to witness and celebrate the abundant grace that pours into ordinary human experience, and the strange and wonderful gift it is to work with God.

God Summons Us

Vocation means that one has been called. At the very least the word conveys some sort of initiative or outreach from one person to another. For Christians, it is God who calls—and the call is not just to some, but to every human being. The call is directed uniquely to each person to become what God has envisioned in creating him or her, and the response to that call will involve the person in the ongoing work of intimacy, harmony, and union between God and all creation.

We have seen that the Benedictine principles for work rest in the earliest Genesis account of the relationship of God and humankind. This is particularly true for vocation, because the first chapter of Genesis makes clear that things begin when God summons forth the created world. God calls "Let there be…" and the call bears fruitful response as the world comes into existence. So we become human beings, each and all, summoned forth by God from no-thing-ness by love. We respond to the divine call in our very being, and potentially all that we are and do is in response to that call. We can imagine that God knows each one of us, knows who we are in love, and knows who we are meant to be in joy. Every day of our lives is a renewed response to this divine knowledge.

Let me emphasize how greatly this vision from Genesis 1 differs from that in Genesis 2 and 3, which is an earlier writer's account of creation. Most of us remember the biblical story of creation as the one given in Genesis 2 and 3, which tries to explain the presence of evil in the world by telling the story of the fall of Adam and Eve, when the serpent urged them to eat the fruit of a forbidden tree. The punishment for this sin is pain in childbirth for the woman, and drudgery in work for the man. God declares in outrage:

> Cursed is the ground because of you; in toil you shall eat of it all the days of your life; thorns and thistles it shall bring forth for you; and you shall eat the plants of the field. By the sweat of your face you shall eat bread until you return to the ground. (Gen. 3:17-19)

Because this is the story most people remember, and the one that is often pictured in art and literature, some Christians are led to think we are meant to suffer in our work. They assume that the continuing effects of our ancestors' sin in the Garden of Eden still shape our daily round, and that we are required to endure the bitter fruit of that sin throughout our lives on earth.

What a contrast! Look again at the delight and generosity of God in the first chapter of Genesis, written some centuries later:

> God created humankind in his image....God blessed them, and God said to them, "Be fruitful and multiply, and fill the earth and subdue it....See, I have given you every plant yielding seed that is upon the face of all the earth, and every tree with seed in its fruit; you shall have them

for food."...And it was so. God saw everything that he had made, and indeed, it was very good. (Gen. 1:27-31)

Both of these accounts have their place in scripture; both merit our reflection and response. That we fall short of our potential, again and again, seems sure, but it is equally sure that we are called to harmonious and joyful intimacy with God—even in our time on earth. Dare we ignore God's invitation to joy? When we begin to consider seriously our vocation, our call to cooperate with God in the ongoing development of the world, we sense a startling shift in our ideas about what human life and work are meant to be. Benedict's Rule holds together both creation images, focusing on call and response, but never being surprised or discouraged by our tendency to fall short.

The central concept of vocation that is now being lifted to its rightful place in Christian spirituality rests on the idea that God has a need and a purpose for each one of us to fulfill. Every single living thing is specially and individually precious to God. There is no other quite like this one, no other which bears the particular "name" of this one, no other who can fulfill this one's appointed place. While it is true that each one's call is in relationship not only to God but to all others, it is also true that God's plan for the fullness of time can be completed only as each one of us takes our special part in it, day by day. Each of us is an original. Each of us is essential.

The Unfolding of Vocation

Vocation is God's daily call to each of us to be what we are, to allow our lives to unfold according to our intrinsic nature, to become what God knows us to be. One metaphor that scripture and tradition have used to express this call is the giving of a *name*. When God names someone in the Hebrew scriptures it means that they are marked in a particular way by God's grace and power—perhaps that the person who is named has grown into what God has created him or her to be, or soon will. For example, in Genesis God changes the name of "Abram" to "Abraham" (17:5). The new name signifies not only a deepened intimacy between them, but also the fulfillment of God's purpose that will take place in and through Abraham's being. Abraham will be the ancestor of a multitude who will be God's people. The giving of a name is very similar to God's potent word in creation: God says, "Let there be..." and creation blossoms forth.

Similarly, at a later point in Genesis, God changes the name of Jacob to Israel (Gen. 32:24-30). After Jacob wrestles all night with a messenger from God at the River Jabbok, the messenger gives him a new name: Israel, "the one who strives with God." At this point in the story we might feel that Jacob is hardly an admirable character—he has stolen his brother Esau's birthright, and is fleeing in terror. Yet at this moment of struggle and fear Jacob demands a blessing and receives it in the form of a new name, which has a strong formative influence on the man he is becoming.

In preaching on the book of Revelation, the nineteenth-century minister and storyteller George MacDonald reflects on our own name as a calling from God:

> To everyone who conquers I will give...a white stone, and on the white stone is written a new name that no one knows except the one who receives it.[2]

MacDonald suggests that God has a "new name" for everyone, but that it cannot be given until we are ready to hear it. Once the name is received, we recognize it as our own; it fits us so well that it seems we have always known who we are. As we live into the name, we accept the part assigned us in God's unfolding purpose for the whole of creation. Simply by being who we are, we contribute as we are meant to the community we share. Furthermore, something about the name we each receive reveals some wisdom about the nature of God's very self that no other name quite can, so as we live into our particular name we reveal to others what we know of God.

To have a vocation is to allow our particular name to unfold. No one is excluded from this mystery, yet not all have discovered it. Most of us have glimpsed a vision of someone we long to be, some work we long to do—something at once very far away and very near that is fulfilling and joyous. This does not mean that if we don't "guess right" about our destiny we will be lost; vocation is more dynamic and more fluid than that, and unfolds over time. Nor is discovering our vocation a self-engrossing exercise that isolates one person from another; although unique, each vocation is interwoven with others for the benefit of all and the glory of God. Being called to receive a new name is not a call away from the world, but toward it. The soul-work of receiving a name is often difficult and painful for us as we try to let go of whatever prevents us from hearing the daily call. Accepting a name sometimes calls us to risk everything, as did Jesus. But responding to our vocation, St. Benedict wrote, also gradually fills our hearts with unspeakable delight (RB Prologue 49).

God's call to us gives a purpose to our lives: we are meant to be attentive to our own distinctiveness so that we can allow the unfolding of our souls in the service of God. Response to God's daily call deepens our awareness of God's knowledge of us, along with our ability to be a beneficial presence in the world. At the core of our being there is no conflict between what we most desire and what God desires for us. In the deep truth of things there is no tension between wholly loving God, self, and neighbor, for the good of one is the good of all. In Frederick Buechner's apt definition, vocation is "the place where your deep gladness and the world's hunger meet."[3]

This is the vision of work which informs the Rule of St. Benedict. Soon we shall explore how this vision is concretely developed in the Rule itself, and how Benedict's insights might help us. But before we do so, let us pause to ask if there is a significant gap between the vision of vocation and the actual work each of us does everyday. The story of a woman named Jeanne might help with our consideration of this question.

Jeanne consults for a computer software firm, and travels throughout the country introducing store managers to the latest software packages of her company. She remembers being a teenager in parochial school and feeling strange about her bent for mathematics because it didn't lend itself to a " religious vocation." Yet over the years, she has discovered in herself a remarkable ability to help people overcome their fear of computers and enjoy using them; she knows she has a vocation to teach others to be comfortable with computers.

Last year Jeanne was sent on special assignment to Australia, where she spent almost three months introducing her company's entire line to a new market. During that period she stayed in the home of a host couple with whom she became good friends. Jeanne fell in love not only with Australia—its people, its wild outback, its rhythms of life—but also with the work she did there. The nature of her assignment meant customers assumed that she was a knowledgeable professional, and Jeanne found that she rose to meet their high expectations.

Her return home was a terrible shock. Back in the States, she was just another junior vice-president with a huge workload piled up on her desk, the object of envy and irritation on the part of her coworkers. Within a week all her reserves had been depleted, and she felt physically ill from too much concentration and too little sleep. Australia seemed like a dream, and Jeanne wondered if she had just imagined her success.

She belonged to a small group at her church that met regularly to talk and pray together, so she decided to discuss it with them and ask their advice. In the course of the conversation she began to glimpse the possibility that the highs—her success in Australia—and the lows—her disappointment with her work in the States—were not opposites, but parts of a whole picture she couldn't quite see. Perhaps her experience in Australia was an authentic experience of vocation, but chiefly a foretaste of something yet to come, a vision given to help draw her toward the future meant for her. But there were specific steps she needed to take in order to be adequately prepared for that future. The present discouragement helped her realistically perceive her current situation and some of the continuing influences she would have to challenge to reach the long-term goal.

Jeanne's group helped her see that the authority she felt in Australia was derived less from what people said about her than from gifts God had given her that she used well. Since that was so, she could gradually teach herself not to be so intensely discouraged (or even encouraged) by the responses of others to her. Instead, in prayer she could concentrate on developing the inner authority God gives her, and let that be her primary guide.

As a result of this insight, Jeanne promised her group that she would set aside regular time to be with Christ and to pray about her vocation. She knows that when she engages in regular prayer, she is far less likely to betray her own hopes and sense of vocation, or to betray others in small and large matters. Jeanne asked her group to remind her of that commitment each time they met. She feels greatly relieved to be undertaking something that requires discipline but is also manageable, and she senses any future decisions—such as whether the United States or Australia will be her permanent home—will unfold naturally, in the context of her ongoing relationship with Christ.

As each of us endeavors to make real a conviction that God calls us to holy work in the context of the life we actually live, we will encounter natural confusion and awkwardness. Bringing the vision of vocation together with the actuality of labor always takes effort, usually with personal vulnerabilities. Support from others who are likewise committed helps us persevere with hope, even in the face of discouragement.

Barriers to Vocation

Work is about violence. This is the conclusion Studs Terkel reached after interviewing scores of Americans for his book *Working:*

> Work is, by its very nature, about violence—to the spirit as well as to the body. It is about ulcers as well as accidents, about shouting matches as well as fistfights, about nervous breakdowns as well as kicking the dog around. It is, above all (or beneath all), about daily humiliations. To survive the day is triumph enough for the walking wounded among the great many of us.[4]

Sentiments like these touch responsive chords in many people for whom work is not a vocation. I recently saw a newspaper article bearing the headline: "Feeling Tense? You're Probably Doing Your Job." While unemployment and underemployment increase, new books advise how to "work smarter" for more money and greater "spiritual" satisfaction. Meanwhile, a review in a national magazine suggests that the movie *Disclosure* painted "a realistic portrait of the modern workplace—full of false camaraderie, anxious rumors, and secret-status warfare."[5] Even comic strips are full of gallows humor about work, such as one that shows a new employer saying, "Congratulations, young man! We've decided to let you waste the greater portion of each day here with us in utter misery" while the employee responds, "Thank you, sir! I'll do my very best to pretend I don't hate you." At all levels of the workforce today many are profoundly cynical about any possibility of meaningful and creative work.

The dehumanizing nature of the contemporary work environment will overwhelm us if we think about it for long, but the possibility for effective change depends in part on a realistic assessment of present conditions. Can we identify specific pressures or problems in our work that mitigate against vocation? What are the barriers to hearing and acting upon our call from God in this place? It is a question for each of us to ponder specifically, but common problems infect most workplaces. What are they?

Although the Department of Labor lists more than twelve thousand jobs, eighty-five percent of all Americans work in less than five hundred major occupations.[6] And while the number of jobs is growing in potentially creative fields, such as medical care, computer programming, and service occupations, actual job openings usually require technologically precise skills gained through training or education. Although the workforce continues to include more women, more people with different racial and ethnic backgrounds, and more older workers, job requirements are still defined in standardized terms. Work is becoming increasingly specialized and technical for many, tending toward the boring, or at least the routine.

Some years ago I was part of a project with a local school district in California that involved matching job interests of high school students with job availability in the metropolitan Los Angeles market. At the time, the students were seeking primarily opportunities for service and face-to-face human contact, while the economy was focused heavily on manufacturing. I was intrigued by the assumption of my colleagues that our primary goal was to redirect the inclinations and skills of the students to match the demands of the economy. No one suggested that at least some effort might be directed toward adjusting market requirements to the dreams and preferences of the students. In the intervening years, however, there has been a shift as fewer manufacturing jobs are available. More than half the new jobs created in the next twenty years are expected to be in health services, business services, and retail trade, occupations that benefit from intelligence and sensitivity, flexibility and compassion.[7]

The problem remains, however, that even service occupations are usually rigidly defined, with the expectation that employees will mold themselves to the job. As people come off assembly lines and instead begin to do more of what only people can do, we still remain stuck in the conviction that job performance ought to be invariable, no matter the abilities, inclinations, and life experience of the people who do the work. Many find themselves in jobs that carry the expectation that top management knows what needs to be done, and how it is to be done, and employees have little or no input. The irony of this state of affairs permeates all sorts of human work—from cab drivers not being consulted in decisions concerning how to reroute traffic through a series of one-way streets to teachers being told what lesson plans they are expected to follow during each week of school. While it is clearly true that the employer has an overall perspective essential to effective operation, it is equally true that the employees usually have sound insight into client needs, as well as the particular wisdom born of their own unique experience of life. It is demoralizing to be consistently "passed over" when policies are set or procedures established.

In short, a serious barrier to vocation in today's workplace is the tendency toward specialization and fragmentation. Employees are generally expected to bring only a small part of themselves into their employment, while other segments of life or personality are rigorously excluded. Little wonder that we feel small and bruised when we are daily stuffed into a box labeled "work"! Modern work tends to fragment us, whereas vocation tends to nurture a sense of self as a whole. Modern work fractures and isolates people, even from themselves, whereas vocation demands that each discover and express fully who he or she is in Christ.

Although rigid job definitions are corrosive of vocation, an equally serious problem is the shifting nature of work today. Those entering the workplace for the first time cannot trust that their jobs will remain unchanged or even exist in the marketplace by the time of their retirement. Mechanical engineers discover a growing shift toward electronics; mathematics teachers find a completely new approach to the learning process is expected of them. Many employees require continuous retraining in order to keep current on basic elements of their jobs, while others find their entire profession being phased out of the economy. With ongoing corporate mergers and "down-sizing" as facts of life, even those who have given a quarter of a century to an employer can be dismissed with only a few weeks' notice. Often those who remain in the smaller workforce anxiously overwork in order to please ever-changing management. Even managers are ruthlessly exposed to capricious corporate demands. Vocation suffers as much from lack of continuity as from inflexibility.

Job definitions that are too rigid or too fluid are demoralizing; jobs that ask too little of us are as dehumanizing as jobs that ask too much. Exhaustion and boredom at work are not opposites, but are different ways of signaling that the human being is undervalued on the job. In too many places employees are treated as interchangeable cogs in the workplace, effectively suppressing the possibility of vocation. The gospel radically challenges this state of affairs, insisting that the Incarnation of God has something to offer: a vision of the sacredness of each life. Jesus reveals a God who cares about each unique individual. Each of us has a particular "work" which only we can do. The call into life with this God means that we dare not allow our work or the work of our employees to be trivialized, for each is meant to contribute to the ongoing work of creation.

As created human beings, we are made for purposeful activity. Unless we are imprisoned or ill, we cannot sleep all day and all night, even if someone were to give us food and water at regular intervals. We desire to be occupied, not solely as a means of livelihood, but also because we are energized by sustained mental and physical effort to overcome obstacles or to meet challenges. Because God's love permeates the natural world, work is a primary way in which human beings can participate in God's intention for the unfolding of grace in space and time. Life is fulfilling and satisfying when it involves exploration and discovery, reflection and choice, flexibility in response and a sense of creativity or generativity.[8]

Yet it seems that most jobs minimize precisely these elements of occupation that satisfy our spirits. It is hard to imagine God's purpose and power in our workplaces, whether it be an office cubicle, hospital room, or retail shop. How seldom our jobs include genuine opportunities for exploration and reflection! Few of us have a sense of choice and flexibility in our day-to-day tasks. Seldom do we actually experience the thrill of generating a response perfectly attuned to need. Jobs usually seem quite separate from vocation, and many of us find it too painful even to seek an integration.

What might happen if some of us simply began to defect in place? What consequences might ensue if, respectfully but firmly, we began to do our jobs as if our personal input mattered? How would it be if we began to live and work as if we really did have a vocation and intended to express it in fidelity to God's call? Could we begin to bring our whole selves into our work—noticing where needs are not being met, experimenting with new combinations of solutions, bringing other life experience to bear, praising innovative ideas in others?

Perhaps we could, if it depended only on us. But we may object that workers themselves are helpless to deal with this sort of problem. Employers have all the clout: they can hire and fire; they promote or demote; if their standards are not met, they have every right to reject the worker. This situation came home to me at a recent dinner party, which started late because the host never gets home from work until eight o'clock, even on Saturdays. Over dinner we discussed the recent round of layoffs at his firm, which were not accompanied by any reduction in total workload. The remaining staff, especially at his own middle-management level, felt it necessary to pick up the slack if they didn't want to join their previous employees in the unemployment lines. One of our party urged our host to assert his authority and simply refuse to work such consistently long hours. Two others immediately objected: "That is naive! No one person can fight the system!"

Such objections raise serious and real issues. When good jobs are scarce, salaries low, and expenses high, it is well to be realistic. When there are children to support and a mortgage to pay, risk-taking at work can have distressing consequences. Conditions that affect the basic structure of the economy itself are best addressed by coalitions of people, public service organizations, and united church groups addressing top-level decision-makers.

Yet that is not the only level at which change can occur. Cumbersome and unjust systems have always existed and probably always will, and they do not voluntarily change themselves. It is only when employees protest dehumanizing conditions that employers are forced to face them. While any one person may not make a difference, the cumulative effect of many such people has considerable weight. We cannot wait for needed structural change to begin living into the call from God which every day comes to each and all of us. There is an opportunity for spiritual conversion within the midst of *every* employment situation, no matter how difficult. In each work situation, we are invited to respond to the opportunity for our own personal conversion, praying that God will use our risks to transform the environment too.

Pursuing our vocation will probably not involve dramatic and life-threatening crises; more likely, we will find ourselves caught up in everyday frustrations. And it is likely that our prayers will invite us to do something a little odd. For example, suppose that a college student knows that the professor expects student papers to contain a paraphrased version of her own opinions, but the student decides to present a well-documented but alternate point of view on the final paper instead. Is it worth the risk of spending the extra time and even then receiving a "B" rather than an "A"? Or perhaps a health insurance employee takes more than the allowed time with a client, helping him present his case for extended hospital time in terms the insurance company can accept. Can she be prepared to counter a possible reprimand courteously, with the reminder that the insurance company's goal is optimum health care and minimizing repeat illnesses? Such actions are relatively small in the grand scheme of things, but they take real courage and help ground us in the deep reason we work, which is to glorify God by being faithful to our true selves and the world's deep hunger. Small but courageous steps will certainly begin to transform us from within and they may contribute to the gradual transformation of the world.

Benedict and Vocation

St. Benedict's Rule gives us a way of thinking about work as something that engages our whole being, as a means of responding to God's daily call to each of us to become who we are. Let us now turn to his own writings and ideas in the Rule about work as vocation, and see how they help us think

about our own work possibilities. We will explore the Rule on work as vocation in three parts:
  (a) the value of the individual, especially from chapters 2, 7, and 64;
  (b) the daily (manual) labor, especially from chapter 48; and
  (c) responding to the call, especially from the Prologue.

The Value of the Individual
Benedict tells us a great deal about how to value the individual person, both in terms of being and doing, in his chapters 2 and 64 on the way the abbot or abbess is to lead and care for the community. While these two chapters are explicitly about the qualities that a leader in the monastic community should possess, they implicitly speak about the exercise of leadership among members and thus about the value of the members themselves.

Benedict was a strong advocate of community life: it might almost be said that Benedict's primary legacy is describing how a community of Christians can serve God and the world. But can community be reconciled with the needs of the individual? We often fear that community will swallow up the individual, denying not only needs but basic rights. Benedict clearly roots the concept of vocation in a particular call to the individual, but the person's response will also be of service to everyone. Benedict shapes his view of vocation as meeting both individual and community needs through a series of apparent tensions, or paradoxes. The continuous interaction of creative "opposites" brings life and health both to the individual and to the community. Let's look at this series of paradoxes.

One of the surprising features of Benedict's thought is his disregard for equality as we usually think of it. We generally use the word "equality" to mean uniformity of treatment, thinking that equality means everyone is to be handled identically. We feel we must treat every customer and every employee the same, fearing a lawsuit or some other form of recrimination if we vary at all in our behavior from one person to another. Benedict is not interested in such uniformity, however, because he recognizes that uniformity is not the same as respect for the uniqueness of each person. Uniformity lops off all variation so that all exchanges (and presumably all people) fit into the same mold. In contrast, genuine equality accords respect to every person in a way that takes his or her own distinctiveness seriously.

Benedict starts from scripture's reminders that "whether we are slaves or free, we are all one in Christ" and "with God there is no partiality among persons" (Gal. 3:28 and Rom. 2:11, as cited in RB 2:20). Every person is precious in the eyes of God, and we are to respect him or her accordingly. Then Benedict proceeds from equality of respect to appreciation of differences among people. He sees that people do vary, and that varied treatment is necessary in order to elicit the best from each one. Benedict's monastery is a family of originals—like a room full of exquisite works of art! And Benedict's abbot is to have the qualities of a connoisseur of fine art works; in this case the monastics themselves are the valuable canvases on which God is painting marvelous things.[9]

Benedict wants the abbot or abbess to be discriminating and appreciative of the subtleties of God at work variously in each member of the community. While the head of the community is to avoid favoritism and show equal love to all, this basic equality must be seen in the context of Benedict's requirement that he or she nurture a variety of temperaments in the way that is best for each.

> The abbot should suit his action to the circumstances, mingling gentleness with sternness; showing now the rigor

of a master, now the loving affection of a father, so as sternly to rebuke the undisciplined and restless, and to exhort the obedient, mild, and patient to advance in virtue.... Taking this and other examples of discretion, the mother of virtue, let him balance everything so that the strong have something to strive after and the weak are not dismayed. (RB 2:24-25 and 64:19)

The goal is to assist and guide the development of each and every soul into its own unique splendor, as God sees it. The task of the superior is to admire and honor God's glory in each person, helping to bring out the particular qualities of each which God requires for the wonderful composite divinely envisioned. And although God is the artist, and each created being bears God's mark, the work of the soul's unfolding is a co-creative labor involving each person as a participant with God. The abbot's role is to assist each in discovering how best to cooperate with God in the receiving of one's own name, or vocation.

While the idea is fine in theory, we might object that, though a ballet company may do quite well with a batch of *prima donnas,* no work setting—nor any genuine community—can long survive with everyone doing his or her own thing! Yet Benedict unfolds his paradox in another way. While emphasizing specialized attention for each person, he strongly disapproves of willfulness and personal pride. Benedict's focus on the value of the individual as gift of God has nothing in common with our modern ideas about personal preference, for each monastic's uniqueness is honored within the Benedictine call for personal humility.

While Benedict strongly values the person as sacred gift, he also recognizes that the sacred person, the one "named" by God, needs to be released from layers of irrelevant and even harmful social roles. Most of us have developed psychological defense systems that veil the authentic self; all of us are influenced by the cacophony of voices in consumer society that make us feel it is all right to fill ourselves up with things. Many of us are tempted to "play God," to take on responsibility for things over which we have no control and to try to prove ourselves and our worth by accomplishments. These defense systems often masquerade as personality itself, and humility helps us release any artifice that separates us from the genuine self known in relation to God's call. Thus chapter 7 of the Rule, on humility, has a central place in Benedict's concept of vocation.

While each of us has the highest possible calling, this vocation is often obscured by superficial whims and appetites. Our deep desire to be someone in loving relationship with God sometimes lies buried beneath many external desires thrown up by our psyche desperately trying to fill its own emptiness. The aim of humility is genuinely to hear and respond to the deeper call of vocation by releasing the nonessential. However, the steps listed in the Rule's chapter on humility may seem very hard if not downright foolish to us, at first. The language even grates on us. Benedict asserts that "we are rightly taught not to do our own will" (RB 7:21), and goes on to remind us to guard against evil desires, since death is sometimes not far from delight (RB 7:24). He insists that we love not our own will but rather imitate Christ in doing the will of God (RB 7:32). We are to be convinced that we are "inferior and more common than all," saying with the psalmist, "I am a worm" (RB 7:51-52). If this is vocation, who needs it?, we might exclaim. Surely this is just more of that old-fashioned self-hatred that is psychologically unsound and spiritually crippling!

But let us look again. Maybe a period of radical self-assessment is an essential stage on the way to a true and realistic valuing of our worth. Perhaps humility works in counterpoint to self-absorption, so that we have to accept our creaturely limitations at the same time we appreciate our distinctiveness and value. Benedict's insistence both on the precious unique-ness of each *and* on the need to renounce self-will reveals our particular kind of blindness. For individualism actually dishon-ors the distinctiveness of each created being because it prom-ises what is impossible: that within ourselves we have all the resources we need for joy.[10] It rejects the element of relation-ship that is the center of vocation so that, bereft of the mysterious strength of God's life flowing through our own, we ultimately become alienated even from ourselves. The human spirit is made for fulfillment in union with God's Spirit, and we flounder in restlessness until we become the person we are through God's sustaining love.

Vocation is fundamentally a call to relationship. While the call is directed *to* a particular and unique beloved, it must also come *from* a particular Someone (who is *other*). A voice not our own calls to us daily with invitation. A power from beyond ourselves sends forth a word to evoke a response of shared power. But we must be free to hear the word addressed to us, and sufficiently open to receive God's offer of shared life. Humility enables us to respond to the amazing and loving Other who calls. Becoming who we are is beyond human power alone, although with God we become who we have always longed to be.

Even Benedict's abbot is not all-powerful, but is to work with and for God in his relationships with members of his community. The abbot is like the shepherd of a flock of sheep that is owned by a householder to whom the shepherd is accountable (RB 2:7). The abbess is not allowed to plead lack of resources as an excuse for inaction; she is always to be seeking God, and all things needed will be given to her as well (RB 2:35). Thus vocation is rooted in the strong scriptural theme of relationship with God. God called Israel forth from Egypt and claimed her in a lifelong and faithful marriage; Jesus calls his disciples to come and abide with him. In the gospel of John, two of John's disciples follow Jesus down the road and when they ask, "Where are you staying?" he responds simply, "Come and see" (1:35-39). Similarly, when asked about their way of life, the Benedictine response has always been, "Come and see!" It is an offering of relationship as the way to life.

Perhaps we do not want to see that vocation depends on relationship, or that the unfolding of our unique calling depends on humbly seeking the support of Another. Instead, we think of ourselves as self-sufficient creators and producers, and it frightens us to acknowledge that we cannot manage things wholly on our own. In the long term, however, isn't it more frightening to think that we *must* manage things wholly on our own, for there is no effective help anywhere? When we know who we really are, when humility has done its work with us, then we are ready to participate in this marvelous partnership which is the fullest expression of our being.

A call from God is not primarily a call to *do* something. Instead, it is to be a faithful partner and friend, and from that identity vocation naturally emerges. We do what we are. The idea of call suggests a rhythmic alternation between rest in the Godhead and being sent forth into the world. Vocation implies lifelong and daily intimacy with the divine.

Unfolding Benedict's paradox concerning the value of the individual still further, we see that we must accept God's living presence within us in order to become fully the person our vocation calls us to be. Vocation means having access to our own inner authority, which in turn means living from the indwelling presence of God's Holy Spirit within us. Jesus also models this for us: his humility before God causes him to seek primarily to do God's will, and through humility he discovers and acts from inner authority. The people speak about Jesus with awe: "Who then is this, that even the wind and the sea obey him?" (Mark 4:41) and, "The crowds were astounded at his teaching, for he taught them as one having authority, and not as their scribes" (Matt. 7:28-29). We too are meant to have this authority, not as Jesus Christ had it, but in our own particular way. Benedict's abbot is so called because he holds the place of Christ in the monastery and is addressed by a title of Christ, *abba* (RB 2:2-3). He is to be a living example of one who bears Christ in every thought and action. But the abbot is not the only community member who is to live into this authority; *every* member of the community is to be reverenced as one bearing Christ. "They should each try to be the first to show respect to the other" (Rom. 12:10, and RB 63:17 and 72:4).

As we live into our vocation, as we discover our true name, we find that we have access to an inner authority that is powerful. This authority comes from our deep center, where the Holy Spirit is gradually revealing to us who we are meant to be in Christ, who God has named us to be in the beginning. Our inner authority may be mysterious or even invisible to others, who may not understand it because it is not like the authority that comes with licensing or credentials of any kind. It is the authority of a young child who knows she is loved and reaches out in delight and trust. We see it in a street-car conductor who welcomes each passenger as if to his own home. It is shown by the preschool teacher who gently touches a child's shoulder in passing, murmuring praise for the colors of his finger painting. It is the authority of great freedom and great love.

Vocation in Benedict's Rule, then, unfolds from the first discovery of our uniqueness through the teaching of humility into relationship with God in which our inner authority is found. When all these factors are creatively in play, then vocation blossoms. Even in his great reticence, Benedict finds words to affirm the way vocation bears fruit in inner power and outward love at the end of his chapter on humility:

Having, therefore, ascended all these steps of humility, the person will soon arrive at that love of God which, being perfect, casts out fear: whereby he shall begin to keep without effort and as it were naturally and by custom, all those precepts which he had formerly observed not without fear; now no longer through dread of hell, but for the love of Christ, naturally, through a good disposition and delight in virtue. This God will grant to appear by the Holy Spirit in the laborer, now cleansed from vices and sins. (RB 7:67-70)

Benedict points to this overwhelming grace as the fruit of vocation. The individual gains real value in Christ when the Holy Spirit within has free play, eventually releasing fear and giving delight and authority to be who we are.

Work as the Friend of the Soul
The second important element of Benedict's thought about vocation appears in chapter 48, called "Daily Manual Labor." The first sentence of this chapter is usually translated "Idleness is the enemy of the soul," but our discussion emphasizes the inverse implication, "Work is the friend of the soul." The general attitude toward work in Benedict's time is in striking contrast to the Rule's approach: in the culture of ancient Rome, the ideal of the good life was to work as little as possible. If one had means, slaves were purchased to undertake the necessary work of the household, and leisure was regarded as the ideal. The people who would have been attracted to Benedict and Scholastica's communities were of mixed races and classes; presumably they brought to the monastery their varying assumptions about how life was best lived. Yet Benedict makes no distinction among members of the community beyond the date of their entry into the community and the virtue, or goodness, of their lives (see RB 63 entire, plus RB 62:5-6 and RB 21:4).

Benedict and Scholastica's communities assigned approximately equal parts of each day in manual labor, *lectio divina* (holy reading), and daily prayer. Although the basic framework of the day was provided by the round of common prayer, which nourished the soul, Benedict thought it crucial that his monastics also spend significant periods of time each day in exercise for the mind and spirit (study and *lectio divina*), and exercise for the body (manual labor). He saw this balance as necessary for the fulfillment of all the God-given elements in human nature. Monastics work with their hearts, they work with their minds, and they work with their hands. Benedict's pattern of work ensures that a variety of elements will be at play in interacting rhythms during the day, or at least during the week. The implication is that the divine work cannot be sustained without the development and support of our creaturely good.

Benedict requires that everyone in the monastery take part in the workload. The kitchen service is to be shared by everyone, except the sick and those needed elsewhere, "for in this way greater reward is obtained and love is acquired" (RB 35:2). Working for one another is one important way to strengthen our souls. Each person is to carry part of the load of providing for the basic needs of the community; there is nothing to grieve, even if they must labor themselves to gather in the harvest (RB 48:7). Benedict is saying: don't be distressed because you have to work with your hands. No doubt this policy came as a shock to some of the young nobles who joined Benedict, yet the evidence suggests that, over time, monastics did indeed find it deeply satisfying to do their part in all labor.

"Idleness is the enemy of the soul" (RB 48:1). Today, with our tendency toward constant work and busyness, Benedict's assertion must be carefully assessed. Can we even imagine that work could be a friend of the soul? Yet if work is a vocation, an expression of God's call to us to be whole human beings, human work is a necessary and logical partner of prayer in our total response to God. Work is not unimportant to God, but is an expression of gratitude for the gifts we have been given by God and a way to cooperate in God's purposes. Consider your own work for a moment in this light—not so much in terms of what it makes or produces, but rather as one way in which the power of God for transforming good might be introduced into your work setting. Work is a friend of the soul because it gives me a way to share in the ongoing creative purposes of God. Work is the soul's friend because it helps shape my life uniquely to God's unfolding purpose for us all.

This may seem clear enough until we try to live it out, applying it to our own working environment. Do we realize in what ways the work we do supports the labor of others, and vice versa? Can we imagine that doing our work well and cheerfully is not only an honorable thing, but also one that expands our capacity to love? As you ask these questions of your work, ponder why your answers might be in the negative and what steps you personally might take to change the "feel" of your workplace. Think, too, about how you might want to respond to the hostility or derision of colleagues. Remember that we live in a time when people are praised for having an "attitude"—when it's considered "wise" to insist that the world owes us, not the other way around. If generosity and compassion are to be of lasting value, they must be able to withstand cynicism and despair.

Our own identity is expressed in our making and doing. We do not work to gain identity, but we do express and develop our soul's identity through work no less than through prayer. There is an integral relationship between our being and our doing, and the doing is meant to proceed from our being. Our work is one of the principal means for discovering our own gifts and needs. We discover and become who we are through what we do—that is why work is a friend of the soul. Benedict's chapter on labor is about work in this broader context. The entire chapter emphasizes balance as the stable foundation from which monastics make their daily response to the divine call.

Sometimes we expect our paid employment to be the sole outlet for our needs and capacities for work. Yet our lives must include a balance of activities, and it is a rare job indeed that evokes all that we are capable of expressing. If our paid jobs require primarily work with our hands, we would do well to devote some of our discretionary time to strengthening our minds. If we are paid to work with people, we may wish to consider a regular commitment to quiet time alone and with God. Benedict's Rule suggests that no single activity can satisfy us wholly, that our soul's health depends on regularly attending to all aspects of our God-given being. We also attain an essential detachment from our employment when we express ourselves regularly in some activities for which we are not paid, and even at which we may not be particularly skilled. A rhythmic balance of activities within a week or a month helps us remember that we are more than our work, and that it is we who bring dignity to our work rather than the other way around.

A man I will call Frank teaches special children. In his early work years, he drifted around with his degree in sociology, never quite able to settle down, until he realized that he loves kids. He finds institutions of any kind almost intolerable, and in the early years he allowed his dislike of authority figures to impel him from one setting to another. But as he began to focus more and more on those he really serves—disabled and disturbed children—he was gradually able to settle down and settle in. He has been teaching in one junior high school for over ten years now, and it seems right; he stays put because he has learned this is where he belongs.

Still, Frank struggles with the day-to-day. In parent conferences he sometimes gets angry with the indifference and passivity he sees, and sometimes he could weep for the parents' own difficulties. In staff meetings he occasionally blows up when he senses excessive attention to regulations or trivia. He knows he is not easy to work with, but even more he knows that the system in which he works is soul-destroying not only for him, but for everyone else. Frank does not feel he has yet found a place to stand, a peaceful center from which he can freely be both in trouble and in love.

In talking with a friend about his dilemma one day, Frank remembered a line of Emily Dickinson's poetry: "Tell all the truth, but tell it slant,"[11] and wondered if somehow God was speaking to him through this remembered fragment. Puzzling over it, it occurs to him that there may not be any way he can "solve his problem" by heading straight into it. Possibly he could more readily gain perspective on his work by immersion in some totally other activity, rather than by trying to force his work experience to be something it is not.

For some months, Frank has been dabbling with an interest in opera, but he has never taken it too seriously. Now he considers that he has really enjoyed his absorbed concentration on a score or libretto. He and his opera-buff friend have completely relaxed in the hours they spend going to the opera, preparing for it ahead of time, and talking about it afterwards. He has made friends among many long-dead composers, and is enriched by their insights about life. Opera seems to evoke parts of himself that are seldom called upon at work. And he finds in opera a union of passion and peace that is remarkably soothing to his spirit. Frank promises himself that he will stop treating opera like a mere time-filler, and begin to honor it almost as if it were a spiritual discipline. He chuckles to himself as he thinks of it; it sounds so odd, and yet so inviting. Why not?

If you find that your days are consumed with work, that you get up and go to work, arrive home with barely enough energy to eat, watch a little television, and fall exhausted into bed, then Benedict invites you to make a deliberate effort to include other elements in your life. We lose our effectiveness at anything when we do one thing to the exclusion of all else. Make time for prayer in the morning or physical exercise at noon. Deliberately leave work earlier if you can, even with things left unfinished, so as to arrive home with some energy left for listening to music or for reading or painting. Ask yourself, how am I exercising my body, my mind, and my spirit this week?

On the other hand, perhaps you find that nothing really claims your interest and commitment, that you simply move through time and space without seeming to be connected to anything. In this case, balance may be best attained by making a commitment to one thing, and allowing yourself to move more and more deeply within it, where God's presence may be found. Give yourself a period of time—say, three months—to honor the commitment before you endeavor to assess or evaluate whether it is working for you. If work is really the friend of the soul, then over time it will bring us deep satisfaction as well as serve others.

Work as a Response to Call
The third element of Benedict's thought about vocation shapes the very first verses of the Rule itself, where he begins his summons to life in community with a strong statement about God's call to us. The Prologue of the Rule is full of reminders of the life of faith as a vocation:

> To you, my words are addressed, whoever you are....Let us arise, since the Scripture stirs us up....Our eyes being open to the deifying light, let us hear with wondering ears what the Divine Voice admonishes us, daily crying out....And what does God say? Come, my children, listen to me, I will teach you. (RB Prologue 3, 8-12)

For Benedict, call and response is the primary movement of the spiritual life. He emphasizes life in the Spirit as the response to an invitation; God coaxes and encourages rather than demands. And the call is always toward more life as it is meant to be lived, in relationship with the divine. It is a call into the wholeness intended for and offered to every human being.

Not only does the Rule itself begin with the idea of call and response, this theme is repeated each day in the life of the community. Every day, the second psalm in the first prayer office is Psalm 95, known as the *Venite,* "Come" (RB 9:2). The key verse, 95:8, is spelled out in the Prologue: "Today, if you hear God's voice, harden not your hearts." Benedict reminds his disciples of what the Genesis story reveals, that God's word has an effective and inherent power of its own. It goes forth from God to enable a response in those who hear. God spoke forth creation, and it was so! God's purpose is accomplished by God's very word, even as rain and snow do not return to heaven until they have watered the earth, bringing forth seed for sowing and bread for eating (Isa. 55:10-11). But in order to be powerful the word must first be *received.* Humans always have the freedom to harden their hearts and prevent God's word from finding a home in the soil of their being.

With a single sentence from Psalm 95, Benedict not only reminds his community of God's daily call but also suggests the chief barrier to our response by directing our attention to the story of Exodus. Verse 8 of Psalm 95 is a direct reference to the demands made on Moses by the children of Israel, disgruntled by their days of wandering in the desert after their departure from Egypt. Even slavery in Egypt looked better than the dismal emptiness of the wilderness. The Israelites were quarreling among themselves, asking, "Is God among us or not?" (Exod. 17:1-7). The "hardening of the Israelites' hearts" meant that they failed to be aware of God's presence within the midst of their need. By their lack of attention, they rejected God's ongoing call and were unaware of God's strengthening presence.

Vocation requires that we attend continuously to God here and now. Is God in our midst or not? Can we even imagine that God might be with us as we sit before a computer screen, or check someone's blood pressure, or weld one piece of metal to another? Is God in our midst or not? When we are too preoccupied, or too busy, or too worried to stop and look and listen, we are hardening our hearts, and thus cutting ourselves off from our source of strength and renewal. On the other hand, when we make a point each day to be attentive to God's call, we become more receptive to the truth about who we are and whose we are. We are refreshed and renewed in the very hearing of God's word, vitalized for the day. Whenever we really hear God, we are empowered to respond.

Benedict calls vocation a "labor of obedience," and reminds us that we can depart from God's call through "the sloth of disobedience" (Prologue 2-3). As we will see later on, in chapter four, obedience means listening deeply, with the ear of the heart, so that we are attentive and receptive to God's ongoing call here and now. The foundations of Benedictine life are established in a daily rhythm of listening, responding, and being transformed.[12] In order for us to seek continual renewal through the power of knowing our work to be a call from God, we must take regular periods for quiet reflection in our lives. We must frequently offer to God our uncertainties and joys, and be receptive to God's voice calling to us *this* day about the work in which we are engaged.

Even when we have understood the importance of attentive listening, we may be surprised to hear that we must be attentive, in Frederick Buechner's words, to "our own deep gladness."[13] What is my gladness? What is it that I yearn for? What is my vision? If indeed God does call us forth into being, creating us as an essential part of the whole creation united in Christ, then we will be restless until we begin to live according to our true nature. God's way of inviting us is by planting a longing in our hearts for something we cannot quite attain by ourselves. We are meant to hope for things not yet seen, as a way of moving us in the direction of our part in the creative process, while yet relying on God and others for their contributions. We are meant to enjoy the work for which God created us as a way of attracting and sustaining our commitment to what God needs from us.

Our desire is a reflection, an echoing, of God's desire for us. Benedict urges his community to realize that God's desire is the primary formative reality of our lives (RB Prologue 14-20). When God calls out, "Do you yearn for life?", it may seem that we are supposed to *do* something, as when the prophet Isaiah first found himself in the presence of the Holy and cried out, "Here am I; send me!" (Isa. 6:8). But Benedict's instinct leads instead to the experience of Second Isaiah, who finds God *addressing him,* and saying, "Even before you ask me, I will say to you: Here I am!" (Isa. 58:9 and RB Prologue 18). In our eagerness to do what is right, we may forget that the call of God carries with it the power of response. Our principal gift to offer God is ourselves, our willingness to be the focus of God's desire. God's desire resonates in us like a tuning fork, creating an echoing response by the power of its own vibrations.

So while it is important that our vocation be interwoven with humility, it is equally important that it be attuned to our deep inner desire. In a certain sense, both humility and desire move us in the same direction—toward God. For desire is a kind of partialness we cannot fill; it invites us toward completion beyond ourselves. It is as if there is a space within our being that can be filled only by the fullness of God's very life. God's call in me reveals itself through my own yearning to become something I cannot quite name nor can I quite hide. My deep inner desire or gladness is the guide to God's will for me, and when I have moved deeper than the surface distractions that distort my true inner desire, then indeed I can trust it and follow it joyfully, for it moves me into ongoing intimacy and co-creativity with God.

Notice that the metaphor of call and response focuses the spiritual life in a different way than an exaggerated emphasis on sin and forgiveness. In the latter, there is a sense of chasm between the two parties; in the former, there is intimacy. In the latter, the connection is more contractual and formal; in the former, the experience is of mutual delight. In emphasizing the metaphor of call and response in the Rule, Benedict directs our attention to the astonishing fact that it is the Divine One who initiates intimacy, who seeks us. We are urged to believe in our hearts that there is no more precious thing in the world than each one of us, created by God and called forth into wholeness of being without which the universe is somehow diminished. "What could be sweeter to us than this voice of the Lord inviting us?" (RB Prologue 19).

Exercises in Vocation

1. For an average twenty-four-hour day, estimate how much time you spend on each of your activities: work, prayer, relationships, eating, sleeping, travel, and so on. Consider whether or not some elements of your life are being neglected, while others are overextended. If your time expenditure is out of balance, commit yourself to one small action you can take to move it in the right direction, such as five minutes of silence and relaxation three times a week.

2. What are your dreams, your longings, your deep desires? Write them down. Come back to the same question a week later, writing any deeper reflections which have emerged in

the interim. Repeat this several times until you are in touch with your deepest longing, your deepest call to being. Then offer these longings to God in prayer, also praying God will empower you to become what you have envisioned and help you know the next best step you might take.

3. Do you have a sense of calling for your work? What does it mean to you to be called? If you don't feel called to your work, do you feel called to something else? Try to name and put words on an inner vocation unique to you. What are the feelings associated with this sense of call?

4. What are your gifts? What do you do well, enjoy doing, and find yourself often asked to do by others? Where have you been helpful in the past? What gives you energy? What are your interests? Do you think of yourself as creative? If so, how? Distinguish between gifts you keep to yourself and gifts others seek.

5. What are your opportunities? Ask God to help you "see" opportunities within your present round of activities. Don't overcommit yourself: leave some "space" in your week for reflection and for unexpected things to emerge.

6. Are there values which you feel are fundamental to your work that do not seem to be shared by others or by those in management positions at your workplace? Try to name and describe what is important to you. What ways might there be for you to address work situations you are unhappy about?

7. Evaluate your present work situation in terms of these criteria adopted by members of the Jerusalem Community (a group of lay people living together in central Paris according

to a rule of life which links them to God in service of the poor).
They urge that work be:

a. useful   d. lived as witness to the joy in me
b. well done   e. demanding but not exhausting
c. balanced   f. an opportunity for prayer and care

Are you missing any one of these in your work that you really
wish were there? Is there anything you can do to change that?

8. Reflect on the following statement by Archbishop George
Carey:

> Your Christian baptism lays on you an onerous task to be
> a Christian disciple where you are—in your workplaces,
> social encounters, and, of course, in the home....If we
> accept that God has put each of us in a certain place—be
> it a factory, boardroom, home, college, or wherever—then
> that is the place where we are called to exercise a royal
> priesthood as Christians in the world....What is God call-
> ing you to be and do?...There has never been a greater
> need for imaginative women and men who can be trusted
> to lead us with conviction and wisdom.[14]

What does this statement say? What does it say to you? How
do you agree and disagree? What response are you invited to
make in your life, if any?

9. Consider your present work in terms of its opportunities for

a. curiosity and exploration   c. flexibility and choice
b. leisurely reflection   d. creativity in responses

How much do you need these elements in your work? How
much exists at present? How much room is there for you to
include more of these elements in your present work? Who
could help you think about practical ways to proceed?

Three

Stewardship

Taking Care

Be discreet and moderate in [your]tasks....Balance
everything so that the strong have something
to strive after and the weak are not dismayed.
(RB 64:17b, 19)

When God in Jesus became a worker, the earliest vision
of work in scripture was renewed. Jesus worked with
his hands and the tools of a carpenter during the years of his
early manhood in Nazareth, sharing the daily toil of the small
community of neighbors, taking part in the labors and festivals
and prayers. Jesus also worked as he traveled, teaching and
healing the crowds during the three years of his public ministry.
And he worked by his suffering and surrender during the final,
passionate week of his life. Three different forms of human
endeavor were a part of his life, and all three are marked by
steady and regular times of prayer, and the support of fellow
human beings by his side. Work is always in the context of
prayer and rest, of celebration and sorrow; it is an honorable
and meaningful part of human life.

In his stories and parables Jesus is fascinated by human work, and he frequently uses it as a metaphor for the way God is at work. God is like a woman sweeping her house or a man digging in a field. Jesus speaks of God planting a vineyard, trimming a lamp, harvesting a crop, sewing patches on garments, herding sheep. The work of the tax collector does not escape Jesus' notice, and he has a word of challenge and encouragement even for such a notorious character as Zacchaeus (Luke 19:1-10). Even the prayer which Jesus teaches is centered in benevolent images of work: be with us in the earning of our daily bread, and let us join you to bring about your reign on earth as in heaven.

At least four of Jesus' disciples are working fishermen, and their understanding of discipleship is significantly influenced by the craft of fishing. Over and over, Jesus uses images of fishing to deepen the discipleship of these men, urging them to see the spiritual realities hidden in the physical. Jesus even calls them to "fish" for human souls: seeing their work as evangelists as similar to the work in their boats, involving attentiveness to the nature and habits of those they seek, careful preparation and patient waiting, pleasure in a good catch (Mark 1:17).

The disciples come to know that in Jesus' power, their work will produce abundant results, even after they have lost heart in a long, apparently fruitless endeavor (Luke 5:1-11). The angry waters that seem to hinder their work are calmed by Jesus' presence, and the disciples learn not to be fearful of apparent dangers as long as he is with them (Luke 8:22-25). In a final conversation with his disciples, recorded by John, Jesus shares a meal of fish and bread with the disciples to assure them of his humanity; he promises to share human experience to the very end (John 21:9-13). Jesus teaches that everything in creation bears the mark of God's hand, warranting our reverent attention and responding to our tender com-

---

petence. Human work is a primary means of caring for the world God has given us.

Benedictine spirituality is rooted in Jesus' model of stewardship or caring for the created world, and is an expression of Christ's prayer to his Father for his disciples:

> I glorified you on earth by finishing the work that you gave me to do....And now I am no longer in the world, but they are in the world, and I am coming to you....I speak these things in the world so that they may have my joy made complete in themselves....They do not belong to the world, just as I do not belong to the world. Sanctify them in the truth; your word is truth. As you have sent me into the world, so I have sent them into the world. (John 17:4, 11, 13, 16-18)

As Jesus' disciples, we do not belong to the world, but are sent into it. We are in the world, but not of it. It is not always easy to know what this means in concrete human terms, yet it always begins with a sense of being sent into the world to live and work and love, cooperating with the ongoing flow of God's life into the world.

Embracing Detachment

Benedictine stewardship is not hostile to the world, but has a quality of detachment that actually makes possible the wholehearted appreciation of creation. Stewardship embraces the world, but not uncritically; it requires deep reflection on human experience to align oneself with God at work in the world. An inherent tension is contained in Benedictine stewardship, because it cares both for the good things of the world *and* for the goodness of God, refusing to neglect either one. Stewardship takes a fluid and sometimes awkward middle place, which at best is a golden mean and at worst amounts to indifference.

It is easy to fall away from the creative middle, and Benedictines have been swallowed up by worldly cares as often as they
have been isolated completely from the world. The point is
not that they always succeed, but that they consent to the
discipline of trying to embrace the world for God's sake, of
living in but not of the world.

We can see this discipline in the story of Stephen, who is
the acting director of a state agency. He has worked hard to
get his present job, always sharpening his skills, trying to be in
the right place at the right time, willing to move whenever a
promotion requires it. In the course of his career, he consistently has been an advocate of improvement in the quality of
the environment, and he sees all around him evidence of the
fruit of his work. But the demands of his job have limited his
energy for a personal life, and he is now divorced with no
children. Recently Stephen has begun to wonder whether he
has been making the right choices; he has behaved exactly as
he was taught to, but somehow the rewards of his actions seem
empty. Even the public policies he has shaped are slowly
eroding under new pressures. Yet he doesn't feel he knows
how to change; he is used to setting a goal and heading toward
it one step at a time, but he senses that the undefined thing he
misses in his life cannot be achieved that way. Should he
silence the inner voice of discontent, or try to take some
action?

Stephen begins by spending a weekend at a local monastery, and for a while he thinks that perhaps regular time off is
all he needs. But soon his restlessness returns, and he wonders
if he might actually be called to be a monk. He has heard about
the Ignatian spiritual exercises—a time-tested method of dis-
cerning vocational issues through a thirty-day retreat—and he
arranges to take a month off at a Jesuit center to be directed
in the exercises. To his surprise, Stephen's sense of a call to
monasticism actually diminishes on his retreat, so it seems
reasonably clear that he is not called to the religious life. Yet

his hunger for a vital relationship with God continues to grow, and his retreat director encourages him to take some night courses in theology at a local seminary and see what emerges.

Working full-time and taking night courses is demanding, and Stephen feels that he has almost no time for prayer now. But he continues to see a spiritual director once a month, and in four years manages to complete the coursework for a master's degree. Then he suffers a period of depression, partly because he doesn't know what to do with the "extra" time he now has, and partly because he can't understand how God will "use" his seminary work. He is increasingly dissatisfied with his government job.

As the weeks unfold, Stephen gradually resumes a regular daily rhythm of prayer and a monthly day of retreat. The more he gets in tune with his deepest emotions, the more he becomes aware of a strong current of happiness within him. He is amused to notice that at times he almost feels like a teenager falling in love; God seems so near, and with that presence, the whole world seems fresh and beautiful. He still tends to overwork and has anxious periods as well, but his fundamental equilibrium comes from an overwhelming certainty of God's love. Stephen finds that he is often asked to lead retreats and quiet days, not only at his own parish, but also at neighboring congregations. Several people have also asked if he would be their spiritual director.

Now that he has saved a small nest egg from his long employment with the state, Stephen decides to ask for a year's leave of absence to explore whether he can support himself in an emerging vocation to be a spiritual guide. He knows that historically such people have primarily been men and women in religious orders, and that this is may not be work by which he can support himself. But he thinks it worth exploring and figures the year won't be wasted, no matter what. As the months pass, Stephen establishes contractual relationships with three local churches to provide part-time services for each one: leading workshops, teaching adult classes, and offering spiritual direction. The combined total income is not large, but it is enough to cover expenses. He decides to risk continuing it even after the year is over because of the great satisfaction he finds in the work—he feels he is doing just what he has always been meant to do.

Stewardship means working with God to tend and care for the world, including tending and caring for our own vocation. A steward is a trustee, someone entrusted with the care of something that belongs to someone else. A steward is also expected to account for her actions to the actual owner. The linguistic root form of steward is *wer*, which has the connotation of intent watchfulness or awareness, of guarding or keeping something with awe and respect, of treasuring it.

Stewardship is action in the world that corresponds to the inward monastic work of *lectio divina*. The "holy reading" of *lectio divina* involves careful attention to a very small segment of scripture, allowing it to take form in one's imagination, accepting its touch in one's life, and responding to its invitation for today. Both stewardship and *lectio* focus on "keeping" something carefully. In *lectio,* we keep the word of scripture in our hearts, as Mary kept Gabriel's word to her, "O favored one." To "keep" the word allows us to reflect on it for a time, put it away for a while, and later bring it back for more reflection—a work that provides nourishment for our souls even as it transforms us. Mary's treasuring the word from Gabriel transformed her in time, as Jesus' birth and ministry gave shape to her whole life. In earlier days root vegetables were "kept" in the cellar. To assure their freshness and safety from rot and vermin they were stored in a secure place and visited regularly to examine and turn them. The squash and potatoes would carefully be kept at a constant, cool temperature, and watched attentively over a period of some months, so that they could eventually provide food for the table.

In just this way, the steward is to watch over, protect, and bring to fruition the physical things under his care. Is he responsible for three fields and five barns? While he may delegate the daily care to others, he will be sure not only to obtain regular reports but will also undertake a personal inspection from time to time. Are there unexpected heavy rains? The steward will do all he can to protect the crops, shore up the soil, harvest early, and make necessary provisions to salvage everything possible. Or, in a modern idiom, a home-owner can be called a steward of house and land. She may or may not choose to undertake all the physical labor in the house and yard herself, but as its steward she will regularly assess the need for routine and preventative maintenance, scheduling all that is necessary for the house's upkeep and repair. The house is hers only for a time; eventually it will belong to someone else, and so it is her responsibility to enjoy and pass on a fit and comfortable dwelling. It may seem rather plain and undramatic work, and perhaps not at all what we think of as "spiritual," but these tasks of caring for all we "possess" will gradually create in our hearts the "good soil" that yields a hundredfold in all aspects of our life (Mark 4:1-8).

Many of the chapters of Benedict's Rule are devoted to just these tasks of caring for the necessary things of life, and we will look closely at how he prescribes such work as essential to the service of God. But before we do so, let us again consider how countercultural stewardship actually is, so that we can be prepared to persist in this "little" work, confident that it does support God's emerging realm as well as our own soul's health.

Stewardship and Work in Conflict

Stewardship challenges a "business as usual" attitude in the workplace, since it is rooted in a theology of the Incarnation and recognizes the involvement of a loving and transforming God in the immediate and mundane realities that daily confront us. At its best Christianity "fully recognizes the mystery and the promise of the God of things as they are."[1] This is a God who cares about the creation and continues to be involved with human beings in the work of the creation; thus we know our work is important. We work because God needs our care, even and especially where the world seems furthest from God's touch. Yet we cannot ignore the strong tension this vision evokes between what is longed for and what now exists.

Three pressures in particular dominate the workplace today: individual competitiveness, high-volume production, and radical shifts in technology, changing the nature of work itself. These pressures create barriers that Christians must recognize and challenge in order to be effective stewards in their work.

Competition
The first work pressure is *competition*. Our characteristic emphasis on individual success effectively pits each employee against every other in an intensely competitive environment. As in football or any other competitive sport, only one side will win; the other will lose. The winner is the "better" or "best" unit; it outplays the competition after a long period of exhausting and all-consuming preparation for the single moment of decision, the game. In football as in work, individual prowess is highly valued, along with the ability to sustain routine physical injury without whimpering. Shrewd and quick thinking does come into play but always in the context of time-limited outcomes, so strategies are inevitably designed for short-term payoff. The game is played within certain rules, but the rules can be broken so long as the referees don't notice. Professional players who perform well under these conditions receive enormous salaries for careers that inevitably terminate in early middle-age.

In theory, competition on the job encourages the free play of innovative ideas and offers a spacious arena for the natural selection of the most helpful and adaptive products, but in practice it creates hostile adversaries, allowing a few people to become winners while many are losers. Winners tend to be tough and driven, able and willing to work long and hard. Near-perfect performance is to be quickly achieved and routinely repeated, and may be rewarded generously, but "winners" know they will become "losers" as soon as they lag behind or begin to show age. Loyalty is emphasized but is not mutual, for players who do not perform at a certain level are quickly dismissed. Clever people are rewarded for manipulating the system so as to out-maneuver others, even those on their own team. Organizational goals are narrowly defined and strategies are short-term, so that unquestioned victories can be claimed quickly. Dynamics like these drive such familiar contemporary phenomena as hostile corporate take-overs and aggressive and demanding telephone sales marketing.

Competition invades every aspect of our lives, often in ways we don't recognize. We pay our taxes reluctantly, not thinking of ourselves as part of the government which provides smooth roads, safe homes, and excellent schools. Padding an expense account or taking home office supplies for personal use is so common that employees feel entitled to do so. Contractors take construction short-cuts in order to save money, not considering themselves partners with building owners in creating a safe and beautiful place. Customers rush off with too much change, eager to get away before the clerk notices the mistake. Employers routinely hire part-time employees rather than full-time ones, in order to escape paying medical and retirement benefits. Some of us wouldn't mind being mildly injured on someone else's property so we can sue them for all they are worth. All these daily dishonesties are corrosive to the human spirit, but are the far-from-surprising outcome of the instinctive mutual distrust that competition encourages. It is a sign of how burdened we are by the spirit of competition that we sometimes do not even find such behavior strange. Consider how competition affects our educational system. School teachers are pressured to produce quantitative results regardless of the actual rhythms of the process of learning. In some districts teachers are told exactly what and how much is to be taught during each week of the year, in order to assure that all students are exposed to identical material. Meanwhile, teachers are saddled with a grading system which usually has less to do with each student's actual progress than with the assumption that top grades are always limited to a few. Students learn early on that they are competing with each other for success at their grade level. Excellent teachers become discouraged, feeling more like babysitters or prison guards than facilitators of a human learning enterprise. Too often work is coercion and not care, violence and not vocation.

In other traditional professions, such as law, medicine, and the church, competitiveness often takes the form of a struggle for advancement through a chosen career path. Individuals strive to "make partner" in the best firm, or become the pastor of the largest and most successful churches in the denomination, plotting each move with great care. Consider a man I will call Jim, who can't even remember when he first began to realize that he was meant to be a minister. Married while still in seminary, after a couple of assisting positions he was called to be the head of a small congregation affiliated with a spirituality center and became excited about the possibility of integrating congregational life and spiritual outreach. Meanwhile he and his wife Judy had first a boy, who reminded Jim of himself, and then a daughter, who doubled the chaos of the house. Judy was adamant that Jim carry his share of parenting responsibilities, and at first it was a shock to find himself left alone in the house with two irritable children. Jim consoled himself that the parish seemed to be attracting many new young families, since he and Judy were so obviously centered in their own family life.

As the months and years unfolded, the children grew and Judy went back to work part-time. Jim realized gradually that he loved being a father: being with his kids was an experience unlike anything he'd ever known—certainly unlike the clear, unambiguous theology that had previously formed the focus of his life. Yes, they were noisy and willful, but almost at the same minute the children could ask profound questions about life and death, or climb onto his lap with such utter trust and love. Jim liked the fact that he was the primary parent on the two days a week when Judy worked, and he appreciated the flexibility that working in a small church provided.

After about eight years, Jim's colleagues began to ask him if it wasn't time he moved on to another church. After all, he had his career to think of, and he ought to think about a bigger congregation and a bigger salary. He was a fine preacher, and he deserved more. Jim listened to them and reflected on what they suggested. He looked into several openings, he talked with Judy about it, and he prayed too. And he realized that contrary to "normal patterns," it was not right for him to make a move now. He was just where he wanted to be: he enjoyed this community of people, and he valued what they gave him in terms of time to study and pray, and to be a parent as well as a minister. No other church he knew could satisfy all these aspects of his being, and if people thought him odd for not leaving, well, so be it. He was happy.

Production
The second pressure that dominates our work is *production*. We tend to think of ourselves as *homo faber,* the human maker, the artificer. Who we are is what we make, what we produce. Since the beginning of the industrial era in human history, humans have modeled their work on the work done by machines—speedy, consistent, multiple output in mini-

mum time—and on their ability to dominate and construct the environment. Most work environments are in fact shaped by machines. In a large refinery, if the power generator shuts down even for a brief period, it requires several days to get everything back "on line" and costs the company several millions of dollars; therefore, to accommodate the machines' demands, workers are expected to be on hand twenty-four hours a day. On a smaller scale, think of the chaos caused in a modest-sized office when the computer system shuts down for a day—or even for a few hours. So it is not surprising that the assumptions about human work are more suitable to machines: we expect repetitive, flawless, endless reproduction according to predetermined outcomes. We direct action toward sharply defined, clear-cut successes and we prize single-minded dedication to unambiguous goals.

This mind-set is not limited to manufacturing or business occupations; it has entered professions as dissimilar as health care and publishing. The business administrators of health maintenance organizations and health insurance companies pressure doctors and nurses to provide patients with minimal services in the least amount of time, even when it might cause a later serious relapse. Books on stress reduction are rushed to market, so customers can grab a quick antidote for heavy work demands. Even monasteries find it difficult to reduce expected output—say, maintaining both the bakery and the guesthouse while also keeping a full schedule of prayer—in the face of smaller novitiates and retiring elders. In every area, including human relationships, our primary question tends to be, "What is the bottom line?" Most of our work is shaped by those two four-letter words, "more" and "soon."

The vice-president of a business observes that keeping up in this economy "is a little like trying to shoot ducks—and they are coming off the pond quicker, one after another." But he doesn't resent this; on the contrary, he boasts: "We're all working harder, but at the same time, there's the thrill of victory when you know you've done a good job."[2] Notice how his statements are embedded in the assumptions that production is king, competition is good, individual success and ownership are satisfying rewards. For some people some of the time, this rat race seems creative. But it is enormously costly in human weariness and anxiety, and may indeed be actively sinful. The constant pressure to produce more things may be a barely concealed endeavor to become a little god, rather than to serve God.

Human beings do not function at their best at an intense, frantic pace over long periods. Human beings are normally thoughtful and reflective, raising questions and pondering issues. Our way of working is often trial and error; we do something, correct what doesn't work, and do it again, only incrementally building to a finished product. We learn and change as we interact with matter, ideally guided by the Holy Spirit in a way that enhances our ability to care. Yet the production mentality demands that a task be executed with as little delay or variation as possible. Emphasis on production inevitably limits care, assaults the human spirit, and minimizes God's peace. As Thomas Merton observed, "The rush and pressure of modern life are a form, perhaps the most common form, of its innate violence."[3]

Technological Change

The third pressure dominating the contemporary workplace is *radical change* in the nature of work itself. The irony of the mechanical image of a human worker is, of course, that the workplace itself is less and less like a machine and more and more like a computer chip. The industrial revolution has been superseded by the electronic revolution; no longer is the major output of human work the product, but rather communication. The vast implications of electronic over mechanical technology are now only dimly glimpsed, but already we know that work has passed a major threshold.

One immediate effect of the electronic revolution seems to be a drastic reduction in the number of workers required. Both unemployment and underemployment are major short-term problems of a shifting economy, and many of us have recently experienced sudden and devastating changes in work status and income. Unfortunately, the shift to electronic technology that makes a significant reduction in the workforce possible does not necessarily alter competitive and production pressures in the economy. However, just as the move away from human assembly lines initially reduced the number of jobs, it also created new opportunities for employment of people in more humane occupations. Stewardship involves attention to and interaction with opportunities created by change. Meanwhile, does stewardship offer any solace to those squeezed out in economic transitions?

The underlying principle of stewardship is that our work matters to God. Ultimately we work not to fill in the time, nor to make money, but because we are co-creators with God in the unfolding of the world. Vocation teaches us that each of us has a particular place, a particular set of talents, a particular responsibility that no one else can quite fulfill. God's purposes in history are incomplete if we fail to do our part. This is not to suggest a guessing game in which we have to figure out the "right" answer, nor a contest in which we have to prove ourselves, with God always throwing up roadblocks we have to surmount. The spirituality of vocation and stewardship is not meant to impose an impossible burden or guilt. On the contrary, it intends to reassure us that God is already at work in us, helping us both to find and to follow our special path.

Viewed like this, work becomes a way of acknowledging that, no matter what happens in our lives, nothing can separate us from the love of God. God is always our companion, always working with us to bring unimaginable goodness from even the most distressing circumstances. Stewardship teaches us to seek God's presence and God's purpose in whatever happens. Benedict reminds us that we have tools to shape our inner awareness that our work is meant to embody God's goodness. "Put your hope in God," he writes. "Keep guard at all times over the actions of your life, knowing for certain that God sees you everywhere....And never despair of God's mercy" (RB 4:41, 48-49, 74).

The fluctuating workplace of the electronic age affects those in the workplace no less than those temporarily excluded from the workforce. Although computer chips can assume many of the functions people used to perform, they can also intensify pressures on people's work. The drive toward ever faster computer response may cause workers to feel they too must speed everything up. An overnight flood of messages on fax and voice-mail can create a sense of backlog even before the day begins. Fascination with new technology options can cause hours to pass before eyestrain and back tension are noticed. Competition can intensify in a newly emerging market where everything seems wide open.

Generally speaking, we find that our model of effective work is shaped by the focus of our work. When our primary work is agricultural, the earth and its rhythms are our model of effective activity. When our primary work is industrial, the machine and its products are our model. We do not altogether know what kind of a model the computer chip will create, but it does offer possibilities for work congruent with the values of stewardship, if we trust our vision and take the risks.

One of the principal effects of electronics is the vastly expanded capacity for communication. Information can be readily transmitted between people who have never before met, and world-wide networks of people sharing common interests arise quickly. A pastor in a remote area can have instant access to the latest study on the historical Jesus; monasteries can be informed of and pray for those who are suffering even while a hurricane buffets a coastline far away. The appearance on a home television screen of a beautiful vista in foreign lands can arouse profound awe and wonder, and strangers can feel themselves neighbors.

However, the electronic age has negative potential as well as positive, and it is probable that it too will become dominated by the competition and production mentality if we do not take care. The anonymity permitted in electronic communication can serve to isolate rather than connect, and can be used as a veil for vulgarity and dishonesty. Information without wisdom easily drifts into superficiality. There are enormous challenges in discovering how to be in but not of this newest working environment, cooperating with God.

Clarice is a highly successful real estate broker who specializes in relocating corporate headquarters and has many clients in the Fortune 500 companies. At forty, she fulfilled a life-long dream and obtained a private pilot's license; at forty-five, she moved her family out of the busy metropolitan area to a horse-farm in the hills where her children flourished and her husband enjoyed puttering, while she commuted by private plane into the city twice a week. The family attended a log-cabin church and the teenaged children rode their horses to the midweek Bible study.

Then everything changed: the economy took a tumble and interest rates skyrocketed. Major corporations postponed or entirely abandoned any future moves, and Clarice endured six months without a single commission. The firm's bank had given her a high-interest loan that carried her family for a time, but it was getting increasingly complicated to move funds around just ahead of payments due. She was losing weight and drinking far too much, and there was no end in sight.

One Friday evening, when the pastor and his wife were over for dinner, Clarice passed out, and the paramedics took her to the county hospital for overnight admission. On Saturday, while the doctors were doing some tests, the pastor, Bob, dropped by her hospital room. Weary and weak, Clarice confessed that she had been thinking recently about suicide. She had a large life insurance policy that would pay off the farm mortgage, and she thought her family would be better off without her. She half expected Bob to respond with a lecture about the preciousness of life, and was startled to look up and see his eyes moist. "How hard it must have been for you!" he said—and simply sat beside her for a while in sympathetic silence.

The following Tuesday the pastor came by and they sat together in her study. "Clarice, I think it is important that you and I take seriously what you said to me in the hospital, and I don't think it will just go away now that you're feeling physically better." Clarice nodded, and Bob continued, "I'd like to suggest a couple of steps. First, I want to urge you to talk with your family about how you've been feeling. You don't need to carry this burden all alone, and they may be able to help in ways you can't guess. Up to now you've been imagining what they feel without asking them, and that's not fair to them.

"Second, with your permission, I'd like to talk both with the local banker and the local real estate fellow, both members of our church well known to me. This is just a hick town compared to the circles you run in, but I think you'd be surprised how willing folks here are to help. Give us the chance to try." At first, Clarice was startled and then angry with Bob for interfering. But they argued it out, and in time she agreed.

Financially, things continued to be difficult for Clarice for a couple more years, and she lost her business, yet that didn't matter to her as much as she had feared. She patched together a new job locally, using her business skills in combination with her hobbies, and had developed five acres of their ranch as an exclusive retreat for corporate executives. Income was still erratic and small compared to what she had been used to, but Clarice had more time with her family and her horse. Gradually she began to trust that she was not alone, and in retrospect she wonders if that day in the hospital that felt like death was actually a kind of rebirth.

Tender Competence

How does the God of mystery and promise enter into "things as they are" in contemporary work? In the face of such pressure and stress, how can our work cooperate with God's work? What do we make of the contrast between a vision of work as stewardship and the reality of work as a never-ending cycle of output and competition? While stewardship encourages us to express care in all we do, our work environments all too often mitigate against caring. It would be easier to ignore the Christian vision or to pretend that things are fine as they are. It is painful to hold both in our awareness at once. Yet Benedictine spirituality finds strength in the conviction that God will act through our willingness to live in such tensions.

When we seek help with holding together our vision of stewardship and the reality of work, we often encounter cheerful and encouraging books or speakers who urge, "Work smart!" or, "Do what you love and the money will follow." Such advice, even when offered as a "spirituality" of work, is seldom truly helpful, because fundamentally it reinforces our cultural norms. It suggests that there is something wrong with us because we cannot "get it all together." If only we could cope a little better, or work a little harder, the conflict would disappear. These prescriptions are devastating because they propel us more deeply into individual competition and the drive toward greater production; they do not help us care for our work more effectively.

Stewardship is not the same as coping well or controlling outcomes. We need to be aware that Christian stewardship may require a radical shift in how we understand our work objectives. We *can* effectively challenge our cultural work

---

norms, and carve out a creative way of working for ourselves. Indeed, if we hope to renew our sense of work as a creative and spiritual component of our lives, we must challenge these norms. Yet such challenge is often subtle and difficult, and compounded by real stumbling blocks. Efforts to change are always threatening to the status quo, which tends to deflate or neutralize new visions with routine, lip-service praise and a few more perks.

Anyone genuinely free from the confining and harmful assumptions of the age is perceived as a threat. Jesus' understanding of the sabbath was one expression of such freedom, and it aroused enormous hostility from the religious establishment of his day (Matt. 12:1-14). It is the nature of the gospel to require a kind of death to the old way of living in order to make room for a new way. Whenever we human beings face the possibility of any kind of death, we naturally respond with denial, anger, and an attempt to bargain before we are able to move toward acceptance. Accordingly, those who practice stewardship in work environments hostile to caring will probably be perceived as powerful threats and their ideas greeted with less than enthusiasm.

Generally, we begin the task of bringing care into the workplace with a strong sense of our own vulnerability. To care about something or someone implies that we feel tenderly toward it, and we are sensitive to its needs. Tenderness is quite different from competition; it involves openness to and empathy for the reality of the other. When our tenderness is met with a competitive response, we feel badly used and often bruised. It takes considerable courage to persist with tenderness and caring in the face of hostility—and our courage must be aided by the strength of the Holy Spirit to resist the impulse to slip back into the competitive mode and strike back. It is not necessary for the visionary to escalate demands or become aggressive in response to challenge; it is only necessary to persist, firmly and patiently. Stewardship requires a wise vulnerability, able to endure in the face of opposition.

Yet as stewards we are not limited to vulnerability; we are also the bearers of competence. We have confidence in the power of stewardship to bring about change through God's presence. We may feel vulnerable, but the fact we experience resistance tells us that there is power here, the power of the gospel for new life. As we will see in Benedict's chapter on impossible tasks, we release God's new life into our setting by being willing to persist as stewards. Stewards care even when cynicism is the norm. Stewards are tender where toughness is the standard. Stewards embody competence as friends of God in this place at this time.

Tender competence[4] is a difficult practice, because it challenges the base-line myth of contemporary society that one is either firmly in control or completely helpless. Both control and helplessness are ways of excluding God. If we are fully in charge, there is no place for God's action. If we are completely helpless, we refuse not only God's desire to work in our midst, but also the opportunities before us and our own competence to engage them. Stewardship places outcomes in God's hands, but takes quite seriously the challenge of tender competence in the meanwhile.

The Benedictine way is not dependent upon changing our circumstances, but rather in "refusing to allow our peace, our depth of union with God, to be affected by what goes on around us," according to Cardinal Basil Hume, the Benedictine Catholic primate of England. Whether or not we have the power to change the environment, we certainly can attend to the need for changes within ourselves. "We come to see," Hume continues, "that the difficulties which are the source of our frustrations are not obstacles to union with God but stepping stones to this union."[5]

Benedict always invites us to see things we regard as problems as opportunities instead. God is able to use the worst of difficulties as means to bring about the greatest good. For example, when Benedict's own monastery was destroyed, the monks fled from Monte Cassino to Rome, where they sought refuge first with a monastic brother who was also Pope Gregory the Great, the man who became our only historical source of information on Benedict's life. Stewardship includes an expectation that God will use our faithfulness as an instrument to change the way things are. But we do not need to wait until *things* change in order to do *our own work* of inner conversion. And the wisdom of the stewardship approach to work is that it helps us become aware that the very difficulties which frustrate us are being used by God as means to deepen our understanding and appreciation of life.

Benedictine stewardship is rooted in the scripture-based concept of human work as both materially and spiritually fruitful. In his parables, Jesus favors images of trees giving fruit, or seeds producing grain, evoking images of good soil, warm rain, carefully tended fields. These images of spiritual maturity and vitality are illumined by physical growth toward a purpose that has existed from the beginning. They evoke Isaiah's prophecy in which God declares:

> As the rain and the snow come down from heaven, and do not return there until they have watered the earth,...so shall my word be that goes out from my mouth; it shall not return to me empty, but it shall accomplish that which I purpose, and succeed in the thing for which I sent it. (Isa. 55:10-11)

These images also echo the pattern of Jesus' own earthly life: creativity so focused in God's purpose that its fruit blossoms forth exactly as it was meant to do. Christ's life bears fruit both interiorly and exteriorly in perfect harmony with God's intention. Our lives are similarly meant to come to inner and outer maturity according to God's purpose for us.

However, God's ways are not our ways, and stewardship requires ongoing discernment and fidelity to God. We do not know or see the connections and consequences God understands. The apparent necessity for suffering in each life remains a mystery to us, nor can we imagine resurrection in the midst of our own crises. Scripture and tradition and community are supports in time of trial, but discipline and persistence are required to develop the sense of eager anticipation vital to cooperation with God's transforming power.

For example, consider the personnel manager of a large manufacturing company that systematically hires part-time and contract employees to avoid paying for their health care and Social Security. Observing this pattern, which skirts the law, and knowing the hardship it imposes on many employees of the company, how could a manager best act as a steward of his work? Confronting the company directly is likely to cause the personnel manager to be fired. Calling the Labor Department confidentially is unlikely to produce change because of the difficulty of proving intent to circumvent the law. Organizing the contract employees may be pointless because there are always outside workers who will cross a picket line.

Perhaps such a problem does not seem to be related to Jesus' death on a cross, yet it seems at least arguable that Jesus' death and resurrection were meant to be in solidarity with that manager's personal struggle to discern if and how to act in such a situation. To interpret scripture through the vision of stewardship suggests God's concern with just such specific questions of incarnation, and God's desire to have a human partner with the courage to act in hope of God's power to bring about something unexpectedly good in our midst.

Acknowledging the inner distress caused by this dilemma, the manager begins the steward's work by accepting the tensions of the situation rather than ignoring them, and by praying to experience God's nearness in the midst of those tensions. A first concrete step is to begin gathering data on the long-term costs to the company of high turnover and continuous training of new employees. Watching for opportunities, the manager may find a sympathetic and trustworthy colleague at a professional conference with whom to discuss the problem and potential strategies. Management shifts in the company may create opportunities to rethink several policies, including the preference for contract hiring.

Benedict urges that whenever we begin any good work, we pray earnestly to God to perfect it (RB Prologue 4). Following this guidance, each of us can pray and trust that the God who inspires our desire to be a steward in our specific work setting will also open unexpected doors and windows in what may have appeared to be a proverbial stone wall. However it may feel, we are not alone in this work. We are called each day to create with and alongside God the transformation we cannot yet imagine.

Based on our own situation and gifts, each of us is invited to lead a life illumined by these two factors: a desire to respond to God and a willingness to see daily life as the place where that response is formed. To be Christian is to be called to a life of prayer and work, transformed interiorly by the indwelling of the Holy Spirit, and expressed exteriorly in the midst of the very brokenness and separation which Christ Jesus came to heal. Stewardship is expressed in joyful union with God, both in and beyond the natural world.

The Rule of St. Benedict helps us to expand our understanding of how to be stewards in our own work in the attention given to everyday life. Accordingly, let's turn now to the Rule's guidance about stewardship in work, reflecting on its possible application to our current situations.

Benedict and Stewardship

Benedict's Rule requires that the monastery support itself by its own labor, adding that "the monastery should, if possible, be so constructed that within it all necessities, such as water, mill and garden are contained, and the various crafts are practiced" (RB 66:6). Within a Benedictine community, the normal activities of life would be carried out by the monks themselves. Benedict devotes so much of his Rule to the details of daily life and work that for many centuries large portions of the Rule were considered relevant only to the sixth-century context in which they were written. Today, however, we are realizing that these detailed sections of the Rule can actually reveal to us how all our daily work can be undertaken for and with God.

Benedict shared ideas and even text of his monastic rule with another abbot, known to us simply as "the Master," and both abbots require that the monastics undertake daily labor. However, Benedict and the Master have quite different concepts of why work is important. For the Master, spiritual perfection is the goal, irrespective of time and space, so monastic life focuses mainly on prayer and detachment. The Master allows physical work only reluctantly, because "the body cannot be maintained without the food that sustains it," but he insists that "if possessions are tended with concern and care on our part, they benefit the body, but *they are definitely a burden for the soul.*"[6] If possible, the Master urges hiring someone else to manage "things."

Benedict has a different view. To him care and concern are central to the meaning of work itself, and he emphasizes their importance in matters ranging from clothing to counseling wayward monks (RB 55:7-14; RB 27:1-3). Monastics raise and prepare their own food, make and care for their own clothes, build their own dwellings. Anything assigned to someone is to be treated respectfully, kept clean, and returned in good condition (RB 32:2, 4; RB 55:13-14). If anyone breaks something or loses it or fails in any other way while at work, the fault is to be admitted at once and amends made (RB 46:1-4). These guidelines ensure that all realize that their work actually matters, that what they do and how they do it is important and valued, by God as well as others in the community.

Benedict requires work not only to support the community itself but also to serve others. Christians have always supported themselves as well as cared for one another, and Benedict affirms his reading of the gospel as encouraging and valuing human labor. He links spiritual perfection with the great commandments to love God and neighbor as oneself; therefore monastics are to feed the poor and welcome the stranger. Work is not assigned "simply to prevent his monks from being idle....It is also an obligation towards the neighbor; the monks should earn their living and give alms."[7]

Work also supports the life of faith; a body that is fit and strong is an aid to a sturdy prayer life. Work requires a physical engagement with the world, which discourages preoccupation with one's own sanctity or damnation even as it supports the soul's growth. Sufficient sleep allows food to be fully digested, and lectors at meals are to be given a drink ahead of time so that they do not grow faint as they read aloud from the Divine Word. Benedict recommends a fast until midafternoon on Wednesday and Friday only

> if the monastics do not have to work in the fields and are not inconvenienced by excessive heat....Let the abbot modify and arrange all things so that souls may be saved, and the monastics may fulfill their tasks without any justifiable murmuring. (RB 41:2, 4)

This is a simple and practical guide: fast through the early hours on most days, but be flexible in relation to changes in weather and required work. The objective is not rigid adherence to rules, but growth in a human life on fire with God.

Lest we discount these principles, thinking that monastic work must have been simple and wholesome, unlike the complexity and intensity of modern work, it is well to note that throughout the Middle Ages almost any work of lasting value was undertaken either directly or indirectly by the monasteries. Because the monasteries received gifts of land, they were directly involved in property management, as well as agricultural cultivation and distribution. The monasteries were also the primary keepers and teachers of learning, so monastics tutored children, wrote letters and notarized all manner of transactions, maintained and translated all books of significance, and were centers for medical care. Artistic endeavors of every sort were undertaken by monastics, and they were masters of the latest building techniques and artists of the finest quality in parchment, stained glass, and precious metals.

Monasteries were safe places to stop on long travels, as well as sources of wisdom and counsel for decision-makers, so they always had guests and thus undertook all the work of a hotel, restaurant, and stable. In addition, of course, they had to clothe, feed, and house their own members, with a single monastery often maintaining monastic populations in the hundreds. Finally, they carried out all the special work of both the altar and the almshouse. "During about six formative centuries," writes Dom Daniel Rees, "most of the people who did anything constructive in Europe were either monastics themselves or owed something of their training and culture to monastic communities where the Rule of Benedict was a living reality and an educative power."[8]

Clearly, for many centuries Benedictine principles have been tested in complex and intense work settings, and monastics themselves have not always managed to be genuine stewards of their work, often becoming embroiled in worldly conflicts or refusing to do any work but prayer and chant. Even monastics find it strenuous and challenging to allow their relationship with God to permeate their work. But Benedictines do consent to live in the tension; they are willing to commit to the challenge of seeking the union of God and the world as the only work truly worth doing. Living such a life, they invite us to do likewise.

Benedict's Rule includes many sections which embody ways of thinking about stewardship. Let us select two, chapters 31 and 43, considering each in turn. Chapter 31, "The Qualities of the Monastery Cellarer" is the most complete, as well as the most condensed, chapter of the Rule on stewardship. The cellarer is the official appointed to oversee the collection and distribution of all the goods and materials used in the monastery—business manager, accountant, and treasurer all rolled into one. The cellarer maintains and dispenses tools, monitors the kitchen service and preparation of staple foods such as beer and wine, maintains the clothing cupboard, assures the care of the sick, provides hospitality for any guests, directs needed construction or repairs, and gives aid to the poor. Sometimes the cellarer is actually called the steward; both titles suggest the breadth of the role as manager of the economy for the household of God.

We will explore this all-important chapter of the Rule verse by verse, teasing out Benedict's guidance on the steward's attitudes toward work. As you read the following pages, consider how the steward's work reminds you of your own. To what extent do you direct activities of making or distributing? Are you involved in transactions with people coming to you asking for what they need, sometimes asking for more than you have? Do you have some responsibility for those who are sick, or young, or "strangers"? How do you handle tools, including computers and telephones? Are you involved in food service? Do you build and repair things, or make clothing? Do you have more to do than time allows, and are you able to ask for help? Let Benedict's words speak to you in your own work situation. Be aware as we reflect together that our task is not to apply the steward's qualities to *other people*, determining whether they measure up. We are primarily looking within, asking how fully we ourselves have allowed God's movement in our lives.

The Steward's Qualities

> Let there be chosen from the community as cellarer of the monastery one who is wise and of mature character, temperate, not a great eater, not haughty, nor headstrong, nor offensive, not dilatory, nor wasteful. (RB 31:1)

Two qualifications of the cellarer are immediately obvious: he or she is to be someone chosen from the community and to be someone of good character. The choice from the community may seem obvious, since it is a monastery, but it has important implications for us. To what extent are we active in encouraging one another's growth and celebrating the talents of people with whom we work? When we are familiar with the faults and limitations of others, do we continue to be receptive to their strengths and gifts? Do we provide mutual support for each other not only in common tasks but also in lifelong nurture? When we live and work in the same place for some years, do we still remain open to the Spirit's action within one another, supporting beneficial change? Acknowledging that all fall short of the ideal, we are to seek and raise up leaders among us from those whose lives reveal sound character. We are to treasure those who are actually practicing a life of faith—whose eyes are fixed on God and who are becoming what they behold. Wisdom and maturity are not qualities that can be grasped; they are rather the fruits of a life in which God has been offered space to flourish.

The litany of qualities listed for the cellarer—temperance, moderation in eating and drinking, humility, even-temperedness and generosity, diligence, thrift—are basically summed up in the first: temperance. The cellarer is to be someone who has learned moderation in all things, who is not prone to too much nor too little, but one who enjoys the golden mean. This is a person in harmony with God's rhythms, who does not need to intervene precipitously (trusting that most things will work themselves out in time if they are not opposed too much or supported too little) and who is not fearful of intervening when it seems right to do so (trusting that God will always use honest intentions for good in the long run).

The Steward's Resources

[Let there be chosen one who is] God-fearing; one who may be like a father to the whole community.... Let him have particular concern for the sick, for children, for guests, and for the poor, knowing without doubt that he will have to render an account of all these on the day of judgment. (RB 31:2, 9)

The term "God-fearing" is a qualification for every leader in the monastery. Apparently Benedict considers it an essential quality of spiritual maturity. This may seem strange to us if we associate fear with immaturity; we need to know that Benedict means reverence or awe. It is the fear one might feel out in a small boat in a large ocean, where the immensity and power of the water and sky and wind is overwhelming. Fundamentally, fear of God is the realistic response to Someone infinitely beyond our capacity to comprehend; it is the acknowledgment that God is God, that I am in relationship with Someone greater in every respect than I can imagine.

How does such fear apply to our daily labor? The clue comes in the second part of verse nine, where the cellarer is reminded that "he will have to render an account of all these [in his care] on the day of judgment" (RB 31:9). Essential to the work of the steward is knowing that one is caring for something not one's own, something that belongs to this awesome Other, who will ask us to account for our actions. We may not arbitrarily do anything we choose, for there will be a day of reckoning.

In particular, we are charged with the care of those who cannot care for themselves, the young and the ill, the stranger and those without means. God's love is fundamentally care for those weaker and less complete; we are to emulate this love in our work. What we do matters very much to God, and that is both good and bad news. It is bad news if we are untrustworthy, but it is good news if we do the best we can, and trust in help. Part of being a steward is knowing that we do have access to resources beyond our own, that God is our helper, that none of us need pretend to be complete in ourselves. As Benedict says elsewhere, we "may not complain for want of worldly resources" because "nothing is wanting to them that fear God" (RB 2:35-36). Benedict has deliberately added the phrase from Psalm 34 "those who fear God have no want" here to explain the language he borrowed from the Master's Rule, thereby emphasizing the balance that fear of God provides to the cares of this world by assuring whole-hearted receptivity to God's gifts.

To fear God is to be in relationship with One far beyond us and to know that we are not alone in our work. As Vaclev Havel has said, "The only genuine backbone of all action is responsibility to something higher than my family, my company, or my success."[9] We are genuinely free to act only when we are dependent upon God. The steward is not so much in charge of things as surrounded by wonder and supported by grace. The steward does not fear the attractiveness of good things, because she appreciates them as gifts of God. She is not possessive nor manipulative, but cares constructively and generously for her charges in work shared with God. This is not a hierarchy, with God as the dominant and capricious ruler, but a relationship of mutuality in which the stronger partner gives freely of self for the good of the weaker.

Ironically, fear of God alone enables us to act with authority. As we saw earlier with vocation, true authority comes out of our most essential being, that is, from our deep awareness that we belong to God and are made in God's image. Authority is allowing the divine life to flow through us for our good and the good of others. Fear of God means that all our actions are based on God's own authority—and from fear of God flows our deep stewardship, our care. The steward both takes care and gives it.

The spirit of abundance flowing from trust in—or fear of—God is clearly present in Jason's life. When Jason was twelve years old, he says, he had a vision while weeding his vegetable garden. The trill of birdsong caught his ear, and he peered among the tree limbs to find the source. Suddenly the sun blazed up in a blinding aura, in the center of which stood a draped figure. Jason heard a voice saying, "Seek me," and he seemed to be drawn into a sort of trance in which he could see or hear nothing but the light. After what seemed an eternity, birdsong seemed to awaken him, and he was again in the garden.

Somehow Jason knew not to speak to anyone about what happened. It both thrilled and frightened him, and he was afraid it might happen again. As the days passed, nothing more happened. Yet the vision didn't need to return, because Jason knew he had been singled out—for what, he didn't know, except that it was important. It was not until the middle of his freshman year in college that Jason felt he needed to do anything about the vision. The weekend before, he had gone with a friend to a downtown soup kitchen, and helped feed the five hundred men, women, and children who shuffled through. It really shook him, watching their faces and thinking about the contrast between their life and his own. All day he sat in a hot classroom, watching the fly on the windowpane and only half-listening to the lecture. Suddenly he felt he couldn't bear to spend another minute of his life on such trivia; it was time to "seek him."

Jason's parents were dismayed at his decision to drop out of college and live in the inner city with the kitchen workers. The building the team lived in had no heat and no hot water, and they ate the discarded supermarket spoils along with those in the soup lines. Jason earned the grand sum of ten dollars a month, for "personal expenses." Gradually he felt at ease in the rhythm of life with the kitchen workers. They shared a daily eucharist and a weekly Bible study. Several of them picked up the day-old food at the markets each day, and others chopped up vegetables in the big pots of soup made daily. After a few months Jason even started a vegetable garden on the back lot next to the house.

At the end of the first year, Jason signed up for another year despite the protests of his parents and grandparents, who feared he wouldn't "amount to anything" without a college education. He was realistic about the dangers of life in the inner city, but he had made a choice to share the dangers with those who had no choice about where they would live. He had lived in the community of kitchen workers long enough to know that there were severe personality problems even among those committed to serving the poor. He didn't know what "tomorrow" would bring. But he was living day by day— the way he knew he had to.

The Steward's Charge

> Let the cellarer have charge of everything, but do nothing without the permission of the Abbot. Let him take heed to what is commanded him....Let him have under his care all that the Abbot has entrusted to him, and not presume to meddle with what is forbidden him. (RB 31:3-5, 15)

The phrase here translated "have charge of" is later rendered "care for." Both words lead us back to the crucial term in the creation account: "dominion." What does it mean that humans are given dominion over the earth? What does it mean that the cellarer is to have charge of everything—but within certain limits? Lest we mistake stewardship for ownership, Benedict immediately qualifies the cellarer's role by detailing its constraints and by looking at it in relationship to the superior and, implicitly, to the community and the basic rules that govern its health. Dominion is not power to act without restraint; rather, it is a quality of care defined by the needs of the situation. It is tender competence.

Care is the primary work of the steward, indeed, the primary work of all humans in creation. We tend to think Benedictines renounce all goods and relationships, but the chapter on the cellarer and his or her responsibilities suggest that instead Benedictines are charged to care for things held in common and in trust. Care means neither ownership (this is mine!) on the one hand, nor renunciation of all material things (I have nothing!) on the other. Care, or dominion, means so treating the things of this world with which we are entrusted that we live together in right and fruitful relationship.

In stipulating that even the high-ranking cellarer is to be limited by the orders of his superior, Benedict again reminds us of the fact that stewards are held accountable for the quality of their care. Benedict has already used the phrase "he will have to give account of his stewardship," and seems to be playing on the language of a parable found in Luke 16:1-13, the unjust steward. A steward who has been squandering his master's property is summoned to account for his management. Knowing he will be fired, before reporting to the master he calls in his master's debtors and falsifies their accounts, reducing the amounts they owe, so that after his dismissal they will do him a favor in return. The parable is troubling because

Jesus commends the steward's action to his disciples and seems to value shrewdness more than integrity. Benedict directs us to the parable's deeper meaning by emphasizing that the steward *was* called to account; he squandered property only when he thought no accounting would be required. But when the time came that he had to report, he acted shrewdly, according to the resources available to him. Here Jesus is teaching us to be faithful stewards of our worldly responsibilities, says Benedict, aware that we will have to account for them.

We too must prove trustworthy *with the wealth of this world* if we hope to be entrusted with the wealth of heaven (Luke 16:11). Work is an honorable and essential part of the human condition precisely because it is the means by which we can demonstrate (and learn) the capacity to care for that which has been given to us. This is a spirituality grounded in the Incarnation: God's gifts and our responsibilities are situated in the here and now, however unlikely that may seem.

The Steward's Kindness

Let him not sadden his brethren. If a brother asks him for anything unreasonably, let the cellarer not treat him with contempt and so grieve him, but reasonably and with all humility refuse what he unreasonably asks for....Let him above all things have humility; and to him on whom he has nothing else to bestow, let him give at least a kind explanation, as it is written: "A kind word is above the best gift" (Sir. 18:17)....Let him distribute to the brethren their appointed allowance of food, without arrogance or delay, that they may not be scandalized: mindful of what the Word of God declares he deserves who scandalizes one of these little ones (Matt. 18:6). (RB 31:6-7, 13-14, 16)

How are we to treat those under our care? Benedict speaks of those who have both reasonable and unreasonable claims on us, of those who make demands when we have no resources, of those who depend upon us in many ways. How do we carry out those responsibilities?

Stewards are not to assume or assert total control, nor are they to believe themselves without help. Helplessness arises from the belief that I have no power to influence anything, the belief that nothing I do matters: I am a mere cog in the machine, required to "go along" with the status quo. This helplessness is a lie, however, because whatever the circumstances, we are never far from the help of God. Whatever the circumstances, some choices always remain available to us. However things look, one person's action does make some difference.

Yet many people today feel they have no freedom to stand up for themselves, no freedom to make any changes. Employees complain that management has all the power; managers say that they have to produce a profit for their investors; investors demand that a company keep up with competitors. Public servants explain they have to follow the standards of the funding agency, while funding agencies insist they have to explain to voters where the money goes. Somehow no one seems to feel that they have any authority in the system.

Those who practice nonviolence have long known that firm and consistent resistance, when set steadily against oppression, can be enormously powerful. Taking a stand against even the smallest injustice may be costly in personal terms, but that is a separate question. If we are courageous enough to risk losing some of our "privileges," knowing that nothing can separate us from the love of God, we become very powerful collaborators with God in bringing health into the workplace.

Nonetheless, we must recognize that loss of privilege—whether salary, influence, or even the job itself—can affect us and others severely. For this reason, it is sensible to strategize to gain the greatest leverage for the least risk, rather than rushing in to act without thought. One needs the inner support of a strong life of prayer, with considerable time spent in discernment, testing each step of the way, and the outer support of a few good friends in order to bear the personal costs that may come. But never doubt that there are choices, and that your decision to take a risk is a significant element in your relationship with God. What we fail to do is as important as what we choose to do. We are never really helpless.

Benedict suggests that sometimes the cellarer, when asked for something, is simply to say no—not with annoyance or rudeness, nor as a subtle form of punishment, but simply as a statement of fact. In our own work situation, some requests may be out of bounds or violate our sense of what is right; as we pray and seek discernment, we may find that we have to refuse what is asked. To say yes to some things, we must say no to others.

In our work we sometimes decline to be stewards because we feel helpless and inadequate before the overwhelming social, economic, and cultural powers surrounding us. Christians do work in the midst of all the institutions of our culture, all the centers of greed, all the hot places of violence to people and nature, all the chilling corridors of dishonesty. It is often enormously difficult even to consider potential ways in which we might work as stewards in such environments. Yet there are always ways to create new possibilities and exercise personal authority.

Benedict starts with the simplest of things: do we give a "good word"? In a culture where hurry is endemic and abruptness the normal coin of communication, imagine how much grace can be conveyed by a good, leisurely word. At the lunchtime rush-hour when ten customers are angrily waiting to pay, and one of them yells harshly at the clerk for his stupidity, a sense of impending crisis rises quickly in the room.

A waiter slips quietly to the side of the clerk and whispers a reassuring word in his ear, diffusing his mounting anger and allowing a courteous word to the next customer. This simple exchange is stewardship; it is the presence of God. A receptionist at a car dealership also knows herself to be a steward: she answers up to fifteen telephone calls at a time, each one with a pleasant and personal greeting. She ignores the occasional rudeness, knowing that every caller has a need which can be filled by her colleagues. Does this humble service have any lasting value? In fact, it may have value beyond the price of any car!

Perhaps the vice-president of a company is participating in a series of meetings with the unions and then with the trustees, exploring whether the benefits package can be brought up to par with inflationary pressures. Both the trustees and the union representatives are irritated with her because she hears both sides equally and seeks a fair compromise. She often feels like a football, being kicked back and forth, and yet over time she finds she has earned the respect of both sides.

Or a personnel officer insists that a supervisor honestly confront an employee whose work is below par, explaining exactly what the problem is and helping the employee develop a specific plan to improve in these weak areas over the next six months. The supervisor doesn't want to have the conversation because he feels awkward telling the employee something he does not want to hear; he would rather just fire him outright and let his next employer handle the problem. But the personnel manager has a commitment to every person's development, and knows it is irresponsible to avoid painful conversations.

When we act according to these principles in our work, then we are accepting the authority we do have; we are willing to make ourselves uncomfortable, to insist on giving a good word, and to entrust all outcomes to God's care. "Good word," by the way, means "benediction" (*bene* = good; *dicta*

= word). This is a steward's work, making space for the divine transformation in our midst.

The Steward's Limitations

> Let him be watchful over his own soul, remembering always that saying of the Apostle: he who has ministered well purchases for himself a good standing.... If the community is large, let helpers be given to him, by whose aid he may with peace of mind discharge the office committed to him. Let necessary things be given and asked for at appropriate times, that no one may be troubled or grieved in the house of God. (RB 31:8, 17-19)

Paradoxically, stewardship requires both that we acknowledge we are not helpless and that we are aware of our limitations. Remember the implication of work as vocation: human beings are to act from the deep sense of inner authority that can arise only from relationship with God. We no longer strive to see others as more or less powerful than we because such comparisons are simply irrelevant in God's terms. When we compare our sense of power or helplessness with that of another, we are inevitably captured by the competitive spirit that is so destructive to care. All we need to know is that with God's help, we have enough power for *this moment*. When that knowledge finally becomes part of us, then we do not have to struggle to assure our rightful position; we can generously serve others in joy.

One of the most remarkable characteristics of the Rule is its unfailing accommodation to human limitations, including physical strength. Benedict abbreviates the hours of night prayer during the summer months when the nights are short, for example, so that everyone will have sufficient sleep (RB 10:2); he allows modification of the daily food allowance when work in the fields is heavier than usual (39:6); he insists that relationships be marked by kindness and patience with weakness (34:2-4; 72:5). Above all, he insists that no one is to overwork, so that work may be undertaken calmly and in good spirit (RB 31:17; 53:18-20). Benedict has no need to fear or despise weakness, for he rejoices in reminders that we are always in need of help and care. Weakness helps us remember that our very lives are in God's hands, who gives more generously than we ask. The acceptance of natural limits seems to be a corollary to wholehearted receptivity to the unlimited bounty of God. In a certain sense, it is not until we have accepted our own real limitations that we are truly open to help.

Stewardship starts with an acceptance of our limits; in turn, exploring our limits reveals the extent of our power because limitation opens us to gift. Something in our nature delights in genuine reciprocity; mutuality and trust fulfill us. Through our limitations we learn the pleasure of dependence upon each other. Benedict's Rule makes clear that the cellarer and the abbot must be working as partners for the community's health. Limitations on the cellarer's time and energy require others to join in the work of care and distribution of goods, learning and maturing by their contributions.

Throughout, these reflections on stewardship have been aimed at getting us to reconsider the limitations on human control, and to value human care and compassion for all things. The monastic way is not so much about overcoming limits and changing circumstances as it is interacting with these limitations in such a way as to shape our own soul and strengthen our relationship with God. From the description of the cellarer, we learn about stewardship as caretaking— taking care not only of the tools of our work and the people we work beside, but also of our own bodies, minds, and spirits.

The Steward's Attitude

> The cellarer should look upon all the vessels and goods of
> the monastery as though they were the consecrated vessels
> of the altar. Let him not think that he may neglect anything:
> let him not be given to greed, nor wastefulness, nor be a
> squanderer of the goods of the monastery; but let him do
> all things in proper measure, and according to the bidding
> of his Abbot. (RB 31:10-12)

The first sentence of this section could stand alone as a
summary of stewardship. Let everything you touch be treated
as if it were as precious as the altar vessels. Whenever you
handle any equipment or any person, be reverent. Be full of
care with everything entrusted to you. Everything you touch
or see, everyone for whom you have responsibility, is to be
viewed as something cherished by God, and thus to be
cherished by you.

As we saw in the abbot's care for the vocations of his monks,
care means attending to the inherent qualities of someone or
something, and attending to them in such a way that they are
capable of being useful or creative to their fullest capacity.
Above all, a steward is one who notices and enhances the
essence of a thing, from fruit trees to wooden desks to children
playing. All are valuable and deserving of care, because all are
given by God. The created world is God's gift, and as such we
treat it tenderly. Curiously, this may call for us to be somewhat
more materialistic than we already are, in the sense that we
are to be carefully attentive to the physical qualities of what
we are given in order to husband them effectively.[10]

When you wash the laundry, do you do it grudgingly? Are
the socks thrown in roughly and the towels folded angrily?
When you are driving an automobile, is your mind usually far
away? Do your preoccupations keep you from noticing the
feel of your hands on the wheel, the color of the sky, and the

sight of children playing in an adjacent yard? If an employee seems to be suffering from chronic headaches or skin rashes, do you notice and offer concern? When a particularly fine report is submitted to you, do you immediately begin thinking of the next assignment or take time to express your gratitude to the author? Take a moment now to consider everything that your senses receive during a normal day. Ask yourself, do you treat these papers and pens, these hammers and wrenches, these young children and sick people, as if they were consecrated to God?

Busyness and boredom alike are signs that we have lost touch with the truth of God's radiant presence illuminating everything. When we cease to treasure what lies before us, we reveal the absence of wonder in our lives. The saying "Been there, done that" fundamentally means that we were bored even the first time we tried something, and it takes more and more to entertain and distract us. Boredom and the need to rush are signs of a superficial and passive society; as attitudes, they stand in stark contrast to stewardship.

Whenever I notice that I am either bored or frantic, it is a good invitation to me to pay more attention to where I am and what I am doing, and to reconsider the possibility of a sacred element within whatever is before me right now, no matter how many times I have seen it before. Stewardship emerges from the monastic habit of *lectio divina*, the focused and receptive attention to a long-familiar scripture passage so that it mediates a new and fresh encounter with God in this very moment. The world is God's, and all that is in it bears God's mark; stewardship lies in celebrating this fact.

Work and Prayer United

Like chapter 31 on the role of the cellarer, chapter 43 is also central to an understanding of Benedictine stewardship. It is entitled, "Those who Arrive Late at the Work of God or at Table," and its theme is the continuous interchange of work and prayer in the life dedicated to God. The chapter begins with this admonition:

> At the hour of the Divine Office, as soon as the signal is heard, each one is to lay aside whatever he may be engaged in and hasten to prayer with all speed....Indeed, let nothing be preferred to the Work of God. (RB 43:1-3)

Here Benedict insists that all work is to be continuously intermingled with prayer, in order that work is seen in true perspective. No matter what we are doing when the bell rings for prayer, we set it aside and go to worship and praise. This is a very simple requirement, part and parcel of the daily life of monastics today and throughout the centuries—yet outside the monastery it seems an outrageous intrusion.

Benedict urges that we regularly lay aside whatever we are doing, and turn our attention to God. Deadlines do not matter; they can wait until the work of prayer is complete. It does not matter whether I am in the middle of the most important conference of the decade, I interrupt it for worship. Everything in my work takes its place around the central fact of God's being, adoration of God's mysterious glory, and delight in God's love. Without this centrality of relationship with God, nothing else has meaning. With it, everything else is illuminated with God's generous grace.

It is hard to believe that wasting time with God in this way can possibly be important to our work. It is hard to understand how essential it is that we take time—especially when we are most under stress—to remember that God is, and that we are God's. It is hard to practice anything like this willingness to let the bell "stop me in my tracks" at regular intervals during my day. Yet such a practice is exactly what Benedict requires.

Quite apart from the obvious problem that most of us are not members of a community that joins for prayer at regular and set times throughout the day, an even more fundamental issue often prevents us from taking this requirement seriously. Do I really believe that my relationship with God influences my work in any significant way? Is anything more important to me than finishing the task? If I am in the midst of writing a particularly inspired sentence, what does it take to get me to stop and leave it for a moment? In the middle of a rancorous staff meeting, are we able to take a break, breathe deeply, and ask what God has to do with all of this? With ten elderly people left to bathe and dress this morning, am I willing to stop for five minutes to remember God in my work and be refreshed? Does such an interruption *in the middle of things* really have value, given the difficulty of returning and picking up the work where we left off? It is a serious and difficult question for many of us.

Be honest with yourself. Are you allowing relatively minor problems of where and when and with whom to pray regularly distract you from a serious effort to unite your work and prayer, because you imagine your work to be quite separate from God? Consider dealing with the logistics simply, and explore the possibility of a deeper union of work and prayer. Let's assume we are not talking about long breaks, but merely five to fifteen minutes, say once midmorning, once midafternoon, and once at noon. Let's further assume that we are not talking about trying to organize a group of people, but just to establish a few prayer breaks for our own private use in the midst of our particular work. Is it worth it to us to take a regular break, set our work aside, and remember that God is here and we are God's?

Might it be possible to take a couple of minutes while we work at our desks, turn our chair away from our tasks, sit quietly and concentrate on our breathing, and allow a psalm phrase to rise up in our hearts? Or when the children are tucked down for their afternoon nap, to stretch out on a sofa for a few moments and softly hum a favorite hymn? If we fall asleep, so much the better—God gives to the beloved in sleep (Ps. 127:2)! Some people pray at stoplights; others set aside five minutes after dressing and breakfast but before going out the door to work. In the morning, pretend a prayer bell has rung, and take a moment to acknowledge that this day belongs to God, and know that you will be blessed within every moment of it. In the evening, sometime after dinner and before bedtime, take fifteen minutes to review the day, reflecting on moments both positive and negative and on where God was at those times. There are many ways to dedicate even a few moments to God during the day simply by considering the ordinary brief spaces or transitions as potential prayer moments.

What might be the effect of such a rhythm of "interruptions"? How might such a pattern affect our work? At first it may seem pointless and artificial. But if we persist in the regular practice of prayer breaks in the midst of our work, they are likely to create a powerful shift in our habitual attitudes about our tasks. At first we notice that these spiritual "breathers" have a physical effect: they release stress and give us a slight energy boost. Eventually, interruptions of this sort gradually create in us quite a different sense of the context in which we work, a new perspective on what is really important, and a fresh idea of what we are seeking to accomplish. They might change dramatically how we view our work, giving us among other things a sense both that our work matters to God and also that it is far less urgent than we thought. Because God is always alongside our efforts, we can relax more.

Benedict calls the regular prayer times the *Opus Dei*, "the work of God," and claims that nothing is to be preferred to it. This has sometimes been interpreted as meaning that prayer is the only work of God, and other work is second-class. But as we begin to take prayer breaks in the midst of our work, we may sense another meaning of the "work of God"—that all work is God's work when it is filled with prayer.

Exercises in Stewardship

1. Read the parable of the Unjust Steward in Luke 16:1-13 slowly and reflectively. When you hear the word "steward," what comes to mind? Why is this man called a steward? What might Jesus have meant by this parable? How might the image of the unjust steward apply to your work?

2. Notice the quality of all the physical or material things you touch today. Just for today, let your sense of touch be more acute than usual, and be attentive to the texture and temperature of all you touch. Start with your own skin and clothes; consider your toothbrush, toilet paper, bath towel, breakfast cereal. Be aware of the people you touch during the day: the shoulder jostling you on the subway or an especially warm handshake from an old acquaintance. Do you touch living things such as earth or plants, pets or people? Think about how you are nurtured and numbed, attracted or repelled, by the quality of things around you. Are there any simple changes you would like to make to help you be more aware that you live in a created and not wholly human-shaped world?

3. Take up some project you have done before with your hands, like stitchery or weeding. For the entire time that you are working on this project, be fully present to all the sensory experiences associated with the work: touch, vision, hearing,

smell, even taste. Slow everything down, and enjoy each aspect of what you are doing.

Try this now with something you have never done before. Do you sense yourself being "taught" by the sensory qualities of the thing you are handling how best to handle it? Be aware that the Latin word for "gentleness" is *mansuetude,* related to a root word referring to the hand.

4. For a week, be especially sensitive to encounters you have with your own limitations. Listen to your body, and notice especially any routine distress in your back or joints. How do you react when you find you are unable to complete a task, either on time or at all? When you are sick or weary, what is your response? When you are healthy, what is your response? In an emotional encounter with another person where you feel helpless, try simply to observe both what is happening and how you are responding. Notice the inner messages you tell yourself about your limits. What are you learning by paying attention?

5. Benedict says the abbot is to work in such a way that "the strong have something to yearn for, and the weak nothing to run from" (RB 64:19). What do you think he means?

What are two or three of your weaknesses? How do you deal with them when they surface? What are the limitations which confine you right now? How might they be channels for God's grace to flow into your life? Practice tenderness and moderation with yourself next time you feel weak, and seek help from someone you trust.

What are two or three of your strengths? Do you over-rely on them? How do you periodically "stretch" yourself? How much rest and nurture do you provide for your strong side, as well as "exercise"? What do you "yearn" for? Do you have opportunities to explore and express your yearnings regularly?

---

6. Benedict tells the cellarer that if he does not have enough goods available to meet a request, he is to offer a kind word in reply (RB 31:13-14). What sort of "kind word" might he mean? What would you think if you received a kind word instead of the goods you requested? Can you imagine a situation in which you might choose to give a kind word? How could that help?

7. Recall a previous (not current) work assignment for which you felt helpless and inadequate. Bring to mind the beginning of the assignment—who gave it to you, under what circumstances, and how you felt about doing it. Then consider the resources to which you had access, including your own skills and limitations; recall the actual work you did and the part others played in the outcome. Try to do this recollection without any judgment, just being a fair and objective witness to what occurred.

Looking back, can you see God at work in any way? Does there now seem to be any change or future opportunity that did not occur to you at the time? When you have finished, deliberately turn everything about the experience over to God. If you cannot do this all at once, do what you can and come back later to release a bit more. Entrust it to God's hands as much as possible.

8. Consider and decide on some practice of regular prayer breaks that you would like to try for a period of one month. Be realistic and conservative in the beginning, perhaps starting with five minutes set aside each day at a time good for you—morning, noon, or night. Keep it up for the full month, and then evaluate any effects you notice.

9. Review the stories in which someone provided a "good word" in this chapter. Reflect on them and consider examples

like them of which you know, and discuss the possibilities they suggest with others. Imaginatively apply them to your own life, or take them the next step. What might their effects be, interiorly and exteriorly?

10. Think of a time when you felt deeply cared for, especially a time when you felt very specially attended to. Describe what happened. Who was doing the caring? Where and when? Why did you need another's care? How did you respond? Did you, or can you, think of the caretaker as a channel for God's love to you? Did you find yourself feeling or acting differently after that event? If so, try to describe what seemed different.

11. When your work results in success, do you celebrate? If you do, how do you celebrate? How do you think God looks at celebration? Imagine a possible prayer service integrating celebration of a work success, thanksgiving to God, and praise. Consider writing down the service, and even asking some friends to join you in doing it.

Four

Obedience

Serving One Another

Let us outdo one another in showing honor.
(RB 72:40)

When we begin to consider our work as both vocation and stewardship, we may find that we are increasingly aware of caring for what we have been given. We may have a growing inner sense that God calls us to something, even if it is not our present job. Yet the holiness of work may still seem elusive; our work life may continue to seem far removed from the sacred. Something important is still missing; what else needs to be in place? We have to be realistic about what is possible, we may well tell ourselves. Benedictine ideas about living out our calling or practicing stewardship are fine in theory, but do they work in the real world? Clearly, while vocation and stewardship are necessary elements in a holy view of work, they are not sufficient by themselves. What more is required to experience our work as sacred?

In addition to a sense of call and care, freedom is also central to experiencing work as holy. Or stated another way, sacred work immediately confronts the problem of power. The necessary condition for the sacredness of work is the experience of freedom, of having sufficient power to act in accordance with God's call and gifts. Without the freedom to act, the ideals of "call" and "care" only seem to mock our work. Yet most of us don't control our work. We don't have the freedom or the power to create the kind of work setting that we think is required if we are to be holy workers. We work for and with others, including both hostile and benign bosses who set limits on our choices. True, we can decide how we will respond to any situation, but we often have little choice about the context in which it takes place. We would like nothing better than to give ourselves entirely to our call, but we can't. We are embedded in a network of relationships and responsibilities that make demands on us to conform to normal social expectations.

There are numerous reasons why we do not feel free. We may have real financial constraints that bind us to a certain job: we have to earn enough money to pay for the mortgage, college tuition for our children, or nursing home care for our parents. Or we may hesitate to make any changes in our workplace because we fear that we will have no influence at all in our company if we have a reputation for insubordination. Our freedom may be limited by stockholders who demand a certain level of profit, or by our worry that parents will be outraged if we raise important but "forbidden" topics in the classroom. Occasionally we may feel caught in an overwhelming web of technology where no single decision is clear-cut: an endeavor to be environmentally responsible might require unacceptable layoffs of unskilled workers, for example. The size of our organization may mean we are removed from the centers where decisions are made, and rapid changes in our industry and society that are beyond our control may eliminate long-valued jobs. So we are bound by a number of factors that draw us away from the choices we would like to make.

The remarkable thing about contemporary work conditions is how very few people, even managers, think they have the power and freedom to shape their work. In a time and place where external restraints on individual freedom have been reduced to a minimum, when the actual physical conditions of poverty, disease, and illiteracy have been removed from most lives in our society, freedom in human work still eludes us, since few of us are able to act in accordance with our preferences. We have liberty—external conditions have removed arbitrary limitations from many individual lives—but we do not experience freedom, the ability to act in accordance with our true nature.

This chapter proposes that Benedictine obedience is the key to resolving the problem of freedom and power in sacred work; obedience teaches us how we can integrate liberty and freedom. Obedience can eventually create the inner conditions that release the inner power accompanying true freedom.

Life, Liberty, and the Pursuit of Happiness

The great irony of our lack of freedom is that it emerges precisely from too great an emphasis on individual liberty. American culture is still deeply imbued with the belief that the good life depends on freedom for individual development based upon each person's vision and interests. This belief, which grew out of eighteenth-century political thought, demands radical curtailment of moral restraints on social and economic power in favor of full freedom for private interests. It serenely expects shared rationality and the free play of competing interests to create an harmonious public unity. In pursuit of private interest, it is assumed that everyone behaves morally.

The only legitimate authority is the sum of private needs; the only legitimate authority are those principles to which everyone willingly agrees. When traditional authority has seemed excessively rigid, as it did at the end of the age of monarchy, liberty may seem to require no limits. But a theory which accepts no communal check on individual liberty necessarily reduces legitimate authority to shreds. Inevitably, the rejection of public restraint on individual liberty creates "an inescapable doctrine of contingent anarchy"[1]—in other words, social turbulence and chaos. This emphasis on individual liberty has effectively destroyed our capacity to value authority in community. We believe that if we give up any of our individual freedoms, we will be thrust immediately into an oppressive mass culture that will eliminate creativity. We suffer from the absence of images of authority arising within the shared life. Instead, we imagine ourselves to be isolated units, assuming that no one else shares our desires for a deeper communal life.

Unrestricted freedom eventually corrodes every ongoing association of human beings. Robert Bellah is an articulate contemporary critic of the problems such individualism creates for Christians in the workplace.[2] He emphasizes the continuing influence of the founding myth of the United States in every institution, with its rejection of all limits on individual autonomy other than those to which everyone freely consents. In this last decade of our century, with its insistence on rights and entitlements for every minority point of view, it is not difficult to observe the continued impact of our founding myth. Belief in the absolute rights of the individual, Bellah fears, blinds many Christians to the harsh judgment of competitive and unjust behavior repeatedly expressed in scripture and Christian tradition.

In our churches many people resist the possibilities for spiritual formation and discipline that are offered by shared activities because they fear communal restraints on their personal freedom. Rather than practice ways to communicate through legitimate conflict in order to build consensus in

Christ, we bring competition from the workplace into our encounters at church. Individualism and its consequences make it difficult for us to accept any authority beyond ourselves, and therefore limit our receptivity to the insights on work offered by scripture and tradition.

Our functional model of human community is rooted in an almost mythic celebration of competition, which is often called "the free play of individual interests." The advantage of the free play of fluctuating alliances, sometimes in conflict and sometimes in cooperation, is that it allows the advancement of knowledge and understanding by making room for fresh ideas. But the great and largely ignored disadvantage is that this free play of interest also allows forceful and energetic people to dominate and eventually subdue all rivals. Both of these implications shape our contemporary working environment.

The free play of private interests without limitation is a political and economic theory corresponding to Newton's theory of physics, the way the physical world works. Newtonian physics rejected the classic view of an objective and absolute Authority to which the created world merely conformed. Instead, Newton assigned a critical role to the individual, for he insisted that an objective reality could only be known through its perception by individuals.

Work was understood primarily as a force acting on something. When the individual used perception along with energy, or capacity to work, he or she caused something to happen. The more power the individual had, the sooner the result could be obtained. Work is force; energy is capacity; power is speed. So as each person works without restraint at private interests, he or she inevitably competes with others to obtain more power and energy. Politics blends with physics to create a worldview that assigns high value to personal power, and offers very little support for restraint in the exercise of that power. Psychologically and emotionally, this is still the predominant value system of our culture.

Unreflective application of such standards to experience results in the identification of freedom with the exercise of personal power. Power is defined by the assertion of control; it is jeopardized when divided among too many, for its virtue is the individual's ability to dominate or enforce submission in those who are weaker. Such power assumes scarcity because it cannot be shared, and fears that it will be usurped or replaced. Too often, when we think about individual freedom in our work, we mean the freedom either to master this process better than anyone else or to run away from it altogether.

The Place of Authority and Obedience

These widespread assumptions about power and freedom prevent us from thinking clearly about the meaning of work and its connection to wholeness of life. We focus instead on our sense of powerlessness or our lack of freedom to create the conditions that would enable us to experience work as a sacred task, and we become stuck in these notions because they feed into the dominant mythology and draw us back into its limitations. But there is a different way to approach our frustrations with work, although at first it may seem strange to us: it is through a new valuing of authority and obedience in community, which can open up new ways of embodying freedom in God.

The Hebrew and Christian scriptures assume that the fullest development of the human being is only possible in the context of authority and obedience. Abraham, the father of the nations, is obedient to the call of God to leave his family and home at an advanced age, journeying into the wilderness. Jesus says, "I have come down from heaven, not to do my own will, but the will of him who sent me" (John 6:38).

Benedict follows monastic tradition in urging the centrality of humility in the spiritual life, and in his Prologue to the Rule he exhorts his monks to the labor of obedience to God.

In the Latin and Greek New Testaments, the words for "power" mean "having ability or possibility." Scripture sees power not as strength or force as such, but rather as potency, or essence: the acorn has the power to become an oak tree. Both the Latin *potis/posse* and the Greek *dunamai* mean strength in the sense of capability. God has power to create life where once there was barrenness, for nothing is impossible to God (Luke 1:37). God can save even a rich person, for what is impossible for mortals is possible for God (Luke 18:27). Healing depends in part on the fact that the blind men believe that Jesus *can* heal them (Matt. 9:28).

In scripture, one who is powerful is not primarily a master rather than a slave, but one who has the ability for the task, who is worthy for the work. Jesus turns notions of master and slave upside down when he serves those who call him Lord (John 13:3-17). He models the role of leadership primarily as a guide, one who himself has undertaken the journey before-hand, one in whom we can believe. The New Testament points to this leadership power of Jesus as a guide whose desire is to bring others with him. The Spirit of Truth will *guide* us to the fullness of truth (John 16:13); the Lamb of God will *guide* us to springs of living water (Rev. 7:17).

Scripture prefers the language of authority to the language of power. Authority points toward power as a gift from God; true power comes from sharing the life of God, who is the source of all authority. The emphasis is less on might or command than on a kind of power that is freely given away, for the Source is not diminished but expanded in the sharing. In Latin, the noun used to convey authority is *auctoritas*, stemming from the verb *augere*, similar in meaning to the Greek words *auxein* and *auxo*. The nouns mean "support" or "power conferred" and the verbs means "to make grow" or "to give increase." The authority here is that of an originator or source, one from whom abundance flows out, empowering all it touches. Something augurs well when it carries promise with it. The author of our faith is the one who not only models it, but also gives it freely to others. Only when power is multiplied, as each one claims a share, is the abundance of God's realm manifest. This understanding of power is vastly different from those based on assumptions of scarcity and fear of dispersion. This is genuine authority rooted in bounty, which increases when it is given away.

For Jesus, there is a special Greek word for authority, and it is *ex-ousia:* "out of the essence of being." Jesus taught as one having authority, and not as one of the scribes (Matt. 7:29). Something flowed out from his being that reminded people of God's very self; Jesus was one in whom divine power encountered no impediment as it flowed freely from him, empowering all it touched. The people wondered at this man who taught with such authority: "He commands even the unclean spirits, and they obey him" (Mark 1:27).

The response to genuine authority is obedience. Both the unclean spirits and the dangerous winds and waves *obey* Jesus' authority—*ob-oedire* in Latin, and *hyp-akou* in Greek. Again, both languages convey the sense of being called or bidden by the enabling potency of authority that naturally engages response. This power of authority to bring forth obedience is recalled in the passage from Isaiah cited earlier in connection with vocation:

> For as the rain and the snow come down from heaven, and do not return there until they have watered the earth, making it bring forth and sprout, giving seed to the sower and bread to the eater, so shall my word be that goes out from my mouth; it shall not return to me empty, but it shall accomplish that which I purpose. (Isa. 55:10-11)

Genuine obedience is the natural response to an empowering word, a word so attractive and potent that when it is heard, one also receives the power to respond. Like so many truths about God, this is a paradox. We usually think of obedience in terms of dominance and submission, the forceful imposition of executive will on a resistant opponent. It is hard to imagine obedience as rather like a graceful yielding to the embrace of the beloved. Obedience to divine authority is delighted recognition of something we have always wanted but never before been able to claim; it is receiving that which we have most deeply desired, and it is empowering, too.

When we think of such obedience in relation to personal freedom, all our previous categories seem inadequate. We are reminded of St. Augustine's insight that freedom transcends a sense of personal choice. In a delightful (if confusing!) play on words, Augustine suggests that before the fall, humans were able to sin (in Latin, *posse peccare*); after the fall, we were not able not to sin *(non posse non peccare);* after Christ, we were able not to sin *(posse non peccare);* and in the Kingdom, we will not be able to sin *(non posse peccare).*[3] In other words, the fullest human freedom is the absence of all choice, the freedom not to be able to sin! It seems a contradiction to suggest that freedom functions most fully under constraint; that certain options are actually closed to the genuinely free person. Yet only when we have experienced the liberation of no longer *needing* to make certain choices do we begin to know what freedom really is. The experience of such freedom gives us a whole new way of looking at the limitations in every human life because we can serve God with our whole heart even under the least auspicious conditions.

A systems engineer for a large aerospace company who had participated in a number of highly successful projects over the years was abruptly retired at the age of fifty-five because of major cutbacks in his firm. At first Harry was in shock; when the reality of his loss finally sank in, he became angry. How could they do this to him, after all he had done for them? He flooded the market with his resume, confidently expecting job offers, but as the weeks wore on he realized that the whole industry was cutting back and locally there were no jobs in his field for people of his age.

Harry found it increasingly hard to get up in the morning and watch his wife go off to work. For a while, he too went out each day early—usually to the public library—so the neighbors would think he had somewhere to go. But finally he found himself sitting and watching the television for what seemed like hours at a time.

One Sunday, on impulse, he asked the minister of his church, Paul, if he would come by during the week to talk over a cup of coffee. Harry wasn't quite sure what he wanted, but it felt good to stop pretending things were fine. Paul was sympathetic, so when he challenged Harry to reflect harder on his own reactions to the loss of his job, it came as a surprise. "It's natural to feel angry and depressed in the beginning," Paul told him, "but how do you want to handle this over the long term?"

Harry growled, "I want to get another job." But Paul insisted, "Maybe it's not so much about a future job, as how you respond to what is happening right now. You've got some choices here, Harry. Do you want to let bitterness and self-disgust corrode you from the inside and make life unbearable? Why not pray about it?"

After Paul left, Harry wondered why on earth he had thought talking would help. But Paul's question wouldn't leave him alone: yes, he could taste his own resentment and fear. But what alternative existed? Was there another way to cope with this situation? He prayed. In the beginning talking to God about what had happened to him made him angrier, but he kept on, determined to make God hear him and answer. Then he began to feel things...like what a terrible loss it was to lose his job. It felt just like someone cut off his arm! He had assumed he would always keep doing his work, and it formed the center of all his waking hours. If someone asked, he always answered proudly that he was a systems engineer. What was he, if not an engineer? Was he anything at all?

One day Harry's grandchildren came over for the afternoon, and in response to a question little Harry asked, he went down to the basement with them and made a small house with his electric saw. Little Harry was so pleased that during the following week, Grandpa Harry spent several afternoons in the basement, and began to create a whole village. He'd forgotten how much he loved working with wood as a young man; there had been no time for that in past years. When Harry's daughter said she had kept all the miniatures he had made for her twenty years ago, Harry was pleased.

At first, Harry thought of the woodworking as a distraction from his basic problem because it wasn't bringing in any money, but Paul encouraged him to consider whether God might have had a hand in bringing his woodworking back to mind right now. Harry figured he probably would never know, but he did know he had more energy than he'd had in weeks, and he felt more himself than he had in years. Talking with his wife, they agreed they could try to cut back on living expenses now that their children were out of college, and maybe her salary alone would be enough for now.

For many months, Harry continued to struggle and pray with the question of whether he had somehow failed as a human being by not being gainfully employed. But one morning he awoke and realized it simply was not an issue anymore; he was enjoying life enormously, what with his several volunteer activities and a little money made occasionally by selling his miniatures. At times he was even almost glad he'd been laid off, so that these new doors could open to him.

Freedom Toward God

Scripture and tradition link freedom with authority and obedience because they recognize a distinction between freedom from oppression, and freedom for relationship with God. Since the person's greatest good cannot be known apart from God, freedom *for* something is more important than freedom *from* something. This contrasts with our cultural myth that individual freedom from the demands or constraints of others is the highest value—rather than individual freedom being a way of serving others.

We severely hamper our vision when we view freedom only as the absence of restraint. As Martin Buber has noted:

> For at the opposite pole from compulsion there stands not freedom but communion. Compulsion is a negative reality; communion is the positive reality....Independence is a footbridge, not a dwelling-place.[4]

Full freedom requires an understanding of what it serves. For what purpose do we choose to use freedom? What is its value to us as children of God? Freedom allows us the possibility of choosing to orient our lives around relationship with God. With God at the center, we find ourselves able to work in a variety of ways without the anxiety that might have constrained us. The emphasis of our work need no longer be on production, control, speed, and competitiveness. In time, we discover genuine freedom to live fully even in the face of others' expectations.

It is undeniably true that when we commit ourselves to something—whether it be a job, a value, or a person—beyond ourselves, we have immediately limited ourselves by that commitment. Any commitment curtails our freedom; we agree to certain constraints within which we no longer have full choice. A decision to take a full-time job in one place means we cannot work elsewhere; a commitment to marry one person means that we no longer have the choice to live with another. The fact of human existence means that we are necessarily limited, whether we choose our limits deliberately or not. If we are working at one job full-time, we cannot simultaneously be doing five other jobs, to state the obvious.

One major way we are limited is by the assumptions or perceptions we hold—the windows through which we see the world and our experience. As we have seen, our culture tends to operate from the simple causal, individual-centered Newtonian paradigm in our perception not only of the physical world, but also of our psychological and spiritual possibilities. We think of ourselves as isolated beings, and we think that every individual needs to have everything to which he or she is entitled. For us, the assembly-line view of work, based on unit production by force and speed, has limited our imagination and restricted our ability to experience the inbreaking of the Spirit and to see the importance of the support and care of others in community.

Let us at least choose our commitments rather than letting them claim our lives by default. If we want to shape our freedom for something, then we can begin to search for people we admire and inquire about their choices. No doubt any new commitment will inevitably involve a period of submission to the practices and disciplines which the tradition and community have found best to train (or retrain) our spirits to serve that commitment. For example, Benedict urges that those seeking entry to the monastery have many months and much study in freedom to join the community or to go, but once they commit to the monastery, they are bound to its rules, to its abbot, and to one another (RB 58:9-16). The deeper and more consistent our commitment, the more our "freedom from" narrows, even as we expand in our "freedom to" serve and follow. On the other hand, a commitment rewards us according to the seriousness we assign it. As we commit ourselves to listening to God more and more deeply, we experience the joy of growing attunement to what Benedict called the "Divine Voice daily calling out" (RB Prologue 9).

The Importance of Relationships

In exploring a new way of thinking about freedom for sacred work, we have looked at the role of authority and obedience. The Christian tradition not only emphasizes the importance of obedience to divine authority as the primary purpose of human freedom, but also tells us that authority and obedience naturally bring us into relationship. Relationship with God is inseparable from relationship with other creatures.

Life in community is the primary means by which obedience is learned. The great commandments are to love God, and to love neighbor as self (Matt. 22:37-40); only the Judeo-Christian tradition links individual salvation so intimately to community life. For us, personal freedom reaches its greatest depth of meaning when viewed within a web of relationships. By commitment to one another, we learn something essential from the relational life of God in the Trinity. We discover how the pressure of others' lives actually helps us to become who we are, together in Christ.

If there is one Benedictine principle that towers above all others, it is that Christian life is meant to be lived in community. Although in many ways each of us must work out our own salvation, ultimately God brings us all together to everlasting life (RB 72:12). At some level, we all suffer the failures of our culture; at some level, we all benefit when even a few seek the truth in love. In the chaos of his society, Benedict sensed this no less acutely than we do now. So while Benedict nods to the conventions of his time which encouraged the reclusive life of the hermit, he focuses all the great energy of his Rule on the dynamics of life in community, which he calls "the strong" way of life. Benedict never separated God's call to the individual from God's purposes for all creation. The experience of divine freedom and power requires releasing our fearful hold on individual rights, and opening ourselves to the experience of community. We must be obedient, in the sense of listening deeply, not only to God, but also to one another.

Many of us think of work as the last place we would seek community, and relationships at work are often problematic. But provocative questions are posed if we consider the possibility that we might appreciate the sacredness of our work more rather than less by listening for God in one another and thus being obedient to people and circumstances we cannot control. Every task is embedded in a web of relationships, a network of power and influence. What if we decided to celebrate this fact rather than fight against it? Rather than seeking power over and control in our work environments, we might consider the potential fruitfulness of mutual authority, obedience, and service. Although it is not easy to seek communion and covenant with those whom we have known primarily as adversaries, when we do we participate in freeing God's power for the here and now.

One example of obedience in community occurred for me in writing this book, when my editor disagreed with a chapter I had written. I had submitted a draft, and she asked me to consider a complete revision of one section. I was dismayed, of course, and grumbled about the additional work to friends. But what I found astonishing was that my friends uniformly urged me to resist; they felt strongly that what I had written was mine, and an editor had no business disturbing it. My friends wanted me to send a fiery letter telling her that I stood fast with my original chapter. Implicit in their advice was a denial of the authority of the editor, who was, after all, being obedient to her own vocation to bring forth the best from her authors. There seemed to be no vision among my friends of disagreement in loving respect about text and ideas, disagreement which could produce something better through shared authority than any one person could do. Such a felt absence of a framework of shared authority and respectful disagreement is common to many types of work.

In this case, I chose to try what I am calling the path of obedience, of mutual listening: to take seriously the editor's criticisms, and interact creatively with her suggestions and my purpose in writing and see what emerged. After trying that strategy, it seemed clear to me that the editor was right, and that a much better chapter would result if I collaborated with her suggestions rather than sticking with my first draft, where so many decisions had been made in solitude.

Our culture's primary metaphor for work has been that of the machine, with its grand isolation and rhythms of routine production. In the pre-industrial age, the dominant metaphor may have been the open field, with its patterns of seed time and harvest. In the electronic age, there is opportunity for a new metaphor to arise. Why not that of communication and connection? It may be that the model of relationship is apt in our time, not only from a deeply felt need for alternative values, but also from shifts in the nature of work itself. As we turn now to Benedict's insights about obedience to authority as the means to genuine freedom and power, let us keep this model of interconnection in mind.

Obedience in the Rule

The first step of humility is obedience without delay. This becomes those who hold nothing dearer to them than Christ....As soon as anything is ordered by the superior, just as if it had been commanded by God himself, they are unable to bear delay in doing it.... Such as these, therefore, leaving immediately all that is their concern, and forsaking their own will, with their hands disengaged and leaving unfinished what they were about, with the ready step of obedience, follow. (RB 5:1-8)

The sentences in this beginning of Benedict's chapter on obedience seem to throb with urgency: obedience is to be performed "without delay"; tasks are done "immediately," "as soon as" they are ordered. Benedict wants us to remember the disciples' response to Jesus' call in the gospels, when they left their work and their homes invariably without hesitation. Peter and Andrew leave their father in a fishing boat, and Matthew abruptly departs from his tax collection duties. Benedict tells us that we too are to respond with immediacy and urgency, even to human "orders," as if they had been commanded by God in Christ.

The key to Benedict's thoughts on obedience lies in the phrase "hold nothing dearer than Christ." Obedience is above all a cherishing, an embrace of someone dear. In all that we do, we are to be listening for Christ, discovering Christ, responding to Christ. What a change this makes in the daily round: that we become people preoccupied with preferring Christ in our midst! At this moment, we may be standing in a place that seems far from God—a busy and impersonal airport, a stockyard, an assembly line, a boisterous convention center. But no place is alien to God, and even here we are invited to embrace Christ. Considering this possibility, we can sense an urgency. Surely above all, this place needs the transforming presence of Christ; let me be the one to open the windows to him, so that he knows he is welcome here too!

Preferring Christ is not easy work. Obedience is indeed a laborious task, for it is hard to discern how the voice of Christ could possibly be heard from a profit-greedy manager, a power-hungry corporate vice-president, a violent teenager, or an irate patient. Does Christ in fact speak through all these voices of our working environments, and if so, how? It is often especially difficult to notice the voice of Christ in our co-workers, whom we have already safely categorized in predictable if also troublesome niches. But Benedict insists that we learn to prefer Christ everywhere, especially in superiors and strangers, but also in those who are given to us day by day.

They should outdo one another in showing honor. Let them most patiently endure one another's infirmities, whether of body or character. Let them compete in showing obedience to one another. (RB 72:4-6)

Obedience to Christ in one another means showing honor, being patient with weakness, and listening carefully for deeper truth and wisdom. What makes it possible to give this kind of obedience to one another, even after years of estrangement? Again the key is Christ, and holding Christ dear. I seek to extend to others my generous and willing embrace of Christ, as I hope to receive theirs. I keep looking for ways to love Christ in everyone I encounter at work and everything that comes across my desk. I refuse to be satisfied with superficial impressions because I am searching for Christ in this experience, no less urgently than the woman searching for her lost coin or the shepherd looking for one lost sheep (Luke 15:3-9).

As Esther de Waal points out, "When Benedict reminds me that it is love that underlies obedience, the love of Christ, it becomes easier to make the connection between obedience and freedom."[5] Neither fear nor compliance motivates my obedience. Obedience is not the "easy" work of just doing what someone tells me because I will get into trouble if I don't. Instead, obedience is the active choice to use my freedom to listen deeply to my surroundings and to love Christ there. I obey not because I have no choice, but because I choose to follow the will of God through people and institutions.

The Narrow Way

> And so, as it were at the same instant, the bidding of the master and the perfect work of the disciple are together more perfectly fulfilled in the swiftness of the fear of God. These therefore choose the narrow way, upon whom presses the desire to attain eternal life, of whom the Lord says: "Narrow is the way which leads to life."...Such as these without doubt fulfill that saying of the Lord: "I came not to do my own will, but the will of him who sent me." (RB 5:9-13)

Why would anyone choose the narrow way? Because a desire and a yearning press upon us that has not been eased in the broad road of the status quo. And what is that desire, to what does it call us? Often we are not able to find words to describe what we long for, but occasionally we glimpse a hint of it. Such a hint is given here in Benedict's language about the perfect fulfillment of obedience. The master bids, and the words have not even left his mouth before the disciple is already obeying. This image is similar to Isaiah's picture of God's word as rain, bringing forth growth in the receptive ground.

But have we ourselves ever experienced anything like this simultaneity of request and response? Perhaps if we search our memories we can recall a moment, usually involving someone with whom we have lived long and loved much. The person turns to us and starts to speak, and we have the answer ready before the words are out, so attuned are we to the other. Or perhaps we are alone, longing to share a new insight, and the telephone rings before we have even formed our friend's name in our minds. Sometimes a deceased friend or relative reaches out to us in assurance through a dream. But, we might object, these images are not about *obedience;* they express profound harmony of spirits; they are about love. And yet love is obedience—love that reaches out even to the stranger for the sake of the beloved.

How might such obedience look in the workplace? Sometimes it takes the relatively simple form of showing respect to customers or employees. How easy it is to be disdainful of the "typical tourists" that shuffle through one's beloved museum, of the "undisciplined idealists" who constantly fill the monastery guesthouse, of the unruly students who seem to care little for learning, of the co-workers who often linger to chat while there is work to be done. How important it is to be respectful of the (perhaps hidden) search for meaning that rests in their hearts. An ounce of respectful attention can go a long way toward enabling a stranger to acknowledge the deep call underneath a restless spirit.

But obedience also leads us into much less clear-cut situations. Generally speaking, thoughtful Christians today may be more comfortable with civil *disobedience* than with obedience. True to our American myth, we find it much easier to protest against institutional injustice (the other side of uncritical loyalty) than to live creatively into obedience. Yet too often we disobey *before* we have explored the potential value of obedience, rather than the other way around, because we find it easier to tear things apart than to build them together with God. If we are to take seriously the task of building ongoing healthy communities, then we must learn creative ways of celebrating the valuable as well as removing the harmful.

Obedience functions somewhere between uncritical loyalty and external protest. Obedience—*ob-audire* in Latin—is listening intently to all the factors in a situation, asking where and how Christ might be found and loved here. In obedience, we listen to ourselves, to our bodies, to our sense of inner call, to God's voice within. And we also listen to the whole environment attentively: what is going on here? what is each person bringing to the situation, and what are the possible outcomes? We listen to the "superior" in this context—the boss, the client, the trustees. What is it that they are asking or needing, not only on the surface, but beneath it as well? Sometimes a new perspective can be gained by raising the underlying question that no one has clearly seen but which, once formulated, enables a cooperative solution involving everyone.

We listen attentively and respectfully. We must be realistic, acknowledging the true difficulties or disagreements, but we are not to be cynical; there is always a possibility of a breakthrough beyond anything our own efforts could bring about. Nothing is impossible to God. So in obedience we also listen carefully for God in this situation: where can we see the Spirit moving, and how can we assist or cooperate?

Listening intently eventually brings us to a clear sense of the next best step. We may not see very far ahead, but we can usually see what can be done next. It may not be easy to act in accordance with what we have seen, but trusting in God, we are to obey. For example, a therapist who has been working with a client for a year may sense that the next three months are likely to bring significant breakthrough. However, the insurance company has a rule that it will not pay for more than twelve consecutive months of therapy. The insurance company wants the client to take a break from therapy for six months before resuming for up to another year. An obedient therapist is responsible not to accept the insurance ruling at face value, but to prepare a careful argument in favor of additional work at this time which might well save longer term costs. The therapist might also encourage the client to pay a little higher percentage of the fee for a time if that would help reach agreement. The insurance company and/or the client may not be responsive, but obedient action is not based on whether it causes desirable outcomes immediately. We are obedient because we need to love and serve Christ as embodied here, not as a means to any particular end.

Yet what happens when all possible outcomes become increasingly repugnant to us because the specific work culture in which we participate has drifted too far from our core values? Consider another example: that of a mid-level manager in an airline company who is responsible for maintenance of the company's fleet of planes. In recent years, the maintenance work has been contracted out to the lowest bidder, and the manager gradually becomes aware that the contractor is cutting corners on safety in order to keep profit levels high. When the manager tells his superior about this, he is told to keep his mouth shut because the airline company itself has recently had to reduce fares to stay competitive, and it has no additional money to invest in maintenance. On the surface, obedience would seem to suggest that the mid-level manager would go along with this decision, but how would he then live with himself a few months later if one of his planes crashed, killing a number of people? Clearly, it is not that simple.

Obedience is not the same as turning over responsibility for one's actions to another; it is never indifferent compliance. In his Rule, Benedict has deliberately deleted from the Rule of the Master the line, "What happens among the sheep is the responsibility of the shepherd."[6] In other words, Benedict does not allow the disciple to use obedience as an excuse for undertaking any action that moves away from God. It is God's will we seek, and obedience is a means toward that will, rather than a goal in itself. So, like so many things that we have studied in the Rule, obedience is a paradox. The airline mid-level manager may allow one or even two such top management decisions to proceed without objection, but in time a Christian employee may well be faced with the need to call public attention to illegal or immoral actions that endanger others, and perhaps to seek other employment. Obedience invites us to live in that creative tension which we have come to recognize in Benedictine spirituality: living flexibly in the present moment, seeking to love God there, and doing the best we can.

While there are costs to obedience, there are also gifts. The Rule commends us chiefly to seek obedience's gifts. In the full commitment to Benedictine life, obedience is one of the three major aspects promised in the final vow (RB 58:17). The reason for this is that Benedictine life as a whole is intended to shape us for full enjoyment of our "freedom for" God. We do not at first know *how* to love God with our heart and mind and soul and spirit, but obedience is a wonderful teacher. Obedience allows us to choose to give ourselves to a person and a community and a rule of life we have observed and come to respect and love, so that living among them we can learn to do and be that which we most desire. We must find our way through difficulties and trials and failures, and it helps if we can live in the company of people who are familiar with the territory.

Obedience reveals its primary value in the context of a tradition and a community of people whose way of life makes God more visible for us. Above all, obedience urges that we seek and join such people, either in our work itself, or as a support group helping us live more fully as Christians in our work. It is essential to find a small community of people who, like us, have committed themselves to integrating faith and work, and who will help us to listen intently for God's presence in our own work life. In such a group we listen with others who are also seeking obedience to God, and benefit from shared wisdom. Together, we are able to choose the next best step rather than daydreaming about the impossible or simply giving up. With each other, we know we are supported in prayer and love in a community of obedience.

Wholehearted Obedience

This very obedience will be acceptable to God and sweet to us only if what is commanded is done, not fearfully, tardily, nor lukewarmly, nor with murmuring, not with an answer showing unwillingness.... For if the disciple obeys with ill will, murmuring not only with his lips but also in his heart, even though he fulfill the command he will not be acceptable to God. (RB 5:14-17)

Benedict concludes his chapter with the interior qualities of obedience, making clear that he is not referring to conformity or mere passive acquiescence. Obedience is meaningless if it is given half-heartedly, for it is meant to be a path to God, and what we practice in obedience to one another has much to do with how we serve and love God. Throughout the Rule, Benedict is firm about the trouble created by that ordinary human tendency to grumble, to murmur, to consent outwardly while inwardly feeling superior to the task before us. Grumbling separates us not only from others and from our work, but also from ourselves; we are split between what we do and how we feel. How can we shape our hearts to serve God wholly, when we insist on the divisive tactic of grumbling? Hearing God, we are to serve with our whole heart. This is the work of obedience.

A woman named Margie who enjoys both children and drama quite naturally found herself working in a large church with the children's education programs. Many of her friends urged her to become a minister, but it was not clear to her whether she was called to ordination. Finally she decided to go to seminary and see how she liked it. During the years in seminary, Margie's call gradually emerged so that she was able to return to her Methodist bishop and seek his authorization. While she waited for the normal process of approval to unfold, she resumed work with children's education.

This time, Margie's position on the staff of a church had new meaning for her and she eagerly observed both the lifestyles of the ministers and the expectations of the congregation. After a time, she found it harder and harder to maintain any regular rhythm in her own prayer life, because the church seemed to absorb every waking hour. She loved her work, but she began to resent the fact that it consumed so much of her energy. What was especially discouraging was that all the ministers seemed to suffer from the same dilemma and no one ever had any time off. When even the senior pastor planned a day off, all too often there would be a last-minute phone call that would bring him back into the midst of a pastoral or budgetary crisis. The few times that Margie tried to suggest a staff retreat or to get away for a regular break herself, others seemed outwardly sympathetic but not really serious about actively seeking any real change in the pattern of overwork.

Margie also realized that, while she might be able to function when exhausted, it was difficult for her to act generously at such times. It seemed to her that she was caught in a double bind. She loved to serve and care for people—that was why she sought ordination—but unless she set some time aside to nurture herself physically, emotionally, and spiritually, it was as though she were not truly ministering at all. She mulled over these issues for some months, sometimes angry at others and sometimes upset with herself for needing more time for herself, but always coming back to the core of a genuine desire that would not let her go.

Eventually Margie was ordained and called to a small congregation as assistant pastor. The senior minister was near retirement, and she respected him a great deal and hoped to learn much from him. But she also knew that there was ample opportunity for her to bring her particular gifts to the new job, and she pondered what those might be. She wanted so much to serve; she had waited so long for this. Then a friend reminded her that it was equally important for Margie to think about how she herself would be nurtured in the new job, as well as how she would give. The comment kept echoing in Margie's mind, and as she prayed about it, she realized that she must shape her work, just as it will shape her. And she needed to begin as she meant to continue—with regular daily time for prayer and silent listening to God.

Shortly after her second visit to the new church, Margie looked seriously at the specifics of how to be obedient to her vision. She made concrete plans about when, where, how, and how often she would set aside time with God and put it on her appointment book, and she reviewed them with the senior minister. She thought the plans were good ones, because they took into account her natural rhythms as well as the usual flow of congregational activity, but she knew she would have to pay attention to see if modifications would be needed later. She had no illusions that it would be easy to keep her promise to herself, but she was grateful for having a keen sense of how important this decision was for her and her life with God, and she hoped that would help keep her on track.

Serving One Another

The second major section of the Rule that helps us think concretely about obedience in our work is the chapters on serving one another, chapters 35, 36, and 37. These chapters emphasize the importance of obedient listening in our relationships with others. I often imagine Benedict saying that it is easy to be holy, as long as one lives alone! Others irritate, attract, and make demands on us in ways that force us to see ourselves with "warts and all." Implicit in the Rule is Benedict's conviction that community offers not only support but essential discipline for the soul seeking God.

In these three chapters, Benedict shows how we learn obedience through service to others. We are not ready to accept God's care for us until we are able to care for one another in the practical routines of daily life. We probably cannot view our own neediness as holy until we have served others in need with love. The monastery—like the workplace—is a school for the Lord's service, and we learn to serve Christ by imitating his service to us, by loving one another.

Benedictines understand a primary reason for their daily work as the opportunity to serve and to love. Benedict begins chapter 35, "Weekly Servers in the Kitchen," with the basic principle:

> Let the brothers serve each other in turn...for in this way greater reward is obtained and love is acquired. (RB 35:1-2)

How like Benedict to find an important lesson for spirituality in waiting on tables and serving food! Opportunities abound for Christian love in such mundane matters as eating. In this he is faithful to his study of scripture, in which Jesus so often uses the image of a banquet to speak of God's coming (Matt. 22:2; Luke 12:36), and the new Christian community discovers its first public ministry to the community in the "daily distribution of food" (Acts 6:1). Monastic service is modeled on Jesus' service in love to his disciples. Benedict emphasizes this point by having the kitchen servers begin and end their week of service by washing the feet of all members of the community.

The act of serving, and especially of mutual service, is central to Benedict's thought. For Benedict the servant is fundamentally someone who is bound to another. Benedict gently but firmly draws us ever deeper into relationship with God as we move from willingness to be a "steward"—one of some authority and influence, though working for another (the owner)—to the less acceptable position of servant or slave. He insists that each is to serve the others, and in discussing life together emphasizes Romans 12:10: "Let each outdo one another in showing honor" (RB 63:17 and 72:40). Benedict reflects the ideas of St. Paul, who wrote of being a slave of Christ in the opening salutation of his letter to the Romans and insists elsewhere that he is the slave of those to whom he writes and preaches, for Jesus' sake (2 Cor. 4:5). At first glance it seems a repugnant and unhelpful idea, but we cannot really understand Benedict's teaching without an appreciation of Paul's purpose in using this language.

In Romans 6 and 7, Paul explains why the slave imagery is important to him. He knows that, as baptized Christians, we share in Christ's death and resurrection. Because of this wonderful gift, we are *freed from* the slavery of sin, and *freed to be* slaves of God. We are no longer captive to what previously bound us, but are now free for new life in the Spirit. And this new freedom of life in the Spirit is what Paul means by slavery to Christ.

But, we might object, why trade one kind of slavery for another? Why not be free? Surely it cannot help our progress toward wholeness to be enslaved again, however benevolent our master! Possibly if Benedict found slavery extolled only in the writings of St. Paul, he might have ignored it. But in the gospels themselves there is ample evidence that Jesus himself valued the imagery of slavery.

Many of Jesus' parables are about servants or slaves. In Matthew's account of Jesus' teaching, images of servants predominate throughout the eighteenth to twenty-fourth chapters. Mark 12:1-12 tells of Jesus' parable about the tenants, or servants, who mismanaged a vineyard entrusted to them. Luke also reports many sayings of Jesus about those who serve, such as the slaves ready for their master to return from the wedding banquet (12:35-38). A great deal of Jesus' imagery about the human relationship to God takes the form of stories about those who are in the service of a master. And Jesus does not exclude himself, but describes himself as the servant of all, claiming, "I am among you as one who serves" (Luke 22:27) and "The Son of Man came not to be served but to serve" (Matt. 20:28). John's gospel reports that Jesus washed his own disciples' feet, telling them, "I have set you an example, that you also should do as I have done to you" (John 13:15).

This is hard language for us to take seriously, and no doubt it was hard for Benedict, too. It seems to go against the grain to work so long and hard for freedom only to choose willingly yet another form of servitude. What if the master is unjust? What if the people we serve in Christ's name are ungrateful? What about the importance of disobedience to injustice? What can possibly be the genuine good hidden beneath these difficult words? In society at large, more and more so-called service occupations are undervalued; we think that one serves only if absolutely necessary, and for a short time. Perhaps some people in occupations that are habitually ignored or disdained might receive new dignity in the holiness of their work if we all seriously prayed more with the scripture passages cited.

Benedict has two basic insights about the value of understanding oneself as "slave" in all occupations. The first is embodied in mutual service; the second rests in the concept of freedom *for* something. No one escapes the requirement to serve; everyone must be the servant of everyone else. Rather than establishing boundaries or rules which would enable someone to withdraw from service in cases of oppression, Benedict puts the shoe on the other foot. *Everyone* is to serve, including the one who receives service, so the responsibility for misusing one who serves weighs on the soul of the abuser, who will be required to account for it before God.

Benedict's idea of mutual service is expressed well in chapter 36 on "The Sick." He seems to have in mind the lesson of Matthew 25:35: those who offer even a drink of water in compassion and love are serving Christ in their action. So he insists:

> Before all things and above all things, care must be taken of the sick, so that they may be truly served as Christ himself.... Let the weakness [of the old and children] be always taken into account, and do not allow the full rigor of the Rule as regards food to be maintained in their regard. (RB 36:1; 37:2)

He makes clear that kindness is always to take precedence over law. What might happen if we seriously tried to apply the principle of kindness above law to those inevitable conflicts that occur in our working lives?

The importance of *mutual* service shows through in Benedict's next words, however. Yes, we are to serve generously and fully in love, but service is not meant to be sheer drudgery or fruitless self-sacrifice. Benedict tackles this difficult issue by turning his attention to those who are being served:

> Let the sick on their part bear in mind that they are served out of honor for God, and let them not by their excessive demands distress their brothers who serve them. (RB 36:4)

Charity is required on both sides of the act of service; those who receive service are to do so charitably, no less than those who give it. Just as Christ is both our servant and the one we serve, so we are required to seek Christ both in the one who serves us, and in the one we serve. Everyone is called to grow into Christ; no one escapes the demands of slavery in his name.

But why slavery at all? Why not just freedom to be who we are, and love accordingly? Benedict finds his answer in the distinction between freedom *from* and freedom *toward*. True freedom is the ability to center one's life around what is truly important, so that *every* attitude and choice and action is formed by that center. Mere freedom from restraint can become ungoverned passion, enslaving us. If we think only of freedom from others, without commitment toward a greater Love, all we have done is create a blank space into which more passions can rush, as in Jesus' parable:

> When the unclean spirit has gone out of a person, it wanders through waterless regions looking for a resting place, but it finds none. Then it says, "I will return to my house from which I came." When it comes, it finds it empty, swept, and put in order. Then it goes and brings along seven other spirits more evil than itself, and they enter and live there; and the last state of that person is worse than the first. (Matt. 12:43-45)

We fool ourselves if we imagine we can live with integrity wholly on our own resources, wholly in our own wisdom. Freedom is never solely release; it is also a movement toward commitment.

This "slavery" may even free us to serve God with our whole heart even in the least auspicious work setting. Benedict's Rule encourages this in the chapter on humility, where we are told to "embrace hard and contrary things without growing weary or giving in" (RB 7:35-36), presumably because God's authority can be transforming especially in such inevitable suffering, thanks to our willingness to *choose* what is necessary. We are best equipped to serve one another when we have learned the profound inner power of service to God's Spirit within us. As one wholly committed to Christ, God's slave, we find enormous power to serve one another in love.

Impossible Tasks

Chapter 68 is one of the most interesting in the Rule, for it concerns what to do when asked to do the impossible! How shall I respond when I am required to do what is completely beyond my strength? Benedict could have in mind anything from the ridiculous to the sublime: perhaps I always bake the bread too long; possibly I lack the strength to dig a ditch large enough for the grave of my recently deceased brother; probably I fail again and again to love my enemies. Yet don't we identify with the problem? In every life it happens occasionally that we face a task that we are quite sure is impossible. For us, the issue might be more like complete confusion in the face of the latest computer technology, or great anxiety when we have to address a group of more than six people. But notice that Benedict is quite clear: he is not speaking just of something that requires a little extra effort; he refers to a task that we feel certain is beyond our ability to perform. In that case, the answer seems simple: don't do what you can't do. But if we look a little deeper Benedict's obedience offers a much wiser and more interesting answer than that. He suggests a response in several stages.

First, accept the responsibility. In other words, give it a try. It may indeed be beyond our skill; but perhaps we underestimate ourselves, or something has changed since the last time we tried. So endeavor to do what is asked here and now, and see what happens. Maybe we will be pleasantly surprised and find that we can do it now because it needs doing, and we have been asked. Or maybe we were right, and the task is beyond us; if so, we go to the next stage.

In step two we go back to the person who asked us to undertake the task and explain why we cannot do it. Benedict wisely reminds us both that it is well to select a good time, when the person is feeling relaxed, and to present our case reasonably, without rancor or blame, simply saying, "I find I am unable to do this because...." We summon all our arguments and arrange them clearly, endeavoring to bring the one who has made this claim upon us fully into the picture as we see it.

Perhaps at that point we will be relieved of the assignment. If so, well and good, we carry on with other things. But perhaps there is no one else to do the task, or for some reason our case is not persuasive. Perhaps even after our careful explanation, our request to be relieved of the assignment is denied. We are sent back to try again at the thing we know we cannot do. What then?

Benedict presents us with a very interesting third stage: go ahead and do it! His exact words are:

> If, however, after these explanations the superior still persists in his command, the subject must know that this is best for him; and he is to obey out of love, trusting in the help of God. (RB 68:4-5)

Obey out of love. In this context, to obey means to trust that it is God's very self who commands this thing. And God always empowers what God commands. So we do the impossible not by gritting our teeth nor by sheer will power, but by relaxing—by easing into the task with love and awe, trusting that help beyond our strength will be channeled through us. Maybe we do poorly, or maybe we do well; neither matters very much. What is important is that we consent to be God's instrument in this alien place.

Pondering this chapter of the Rule, we glimpse Benedict's profound and practical conviction that God's presence and help are so very near to us that the possibility of divine transformation is *always* just offstage, awaiting the invitation to renew our daily life and work. But God graciously awaits our call for help before transforming the situation before our eyes. There is something we cannot see, some principle at work that is invisible to us: when we feel most helpless and lost, even when our prayers do not seem to be answered, and when we can admit all this to God and release everything toward God, then we cooperate in the inbreaking of enormous power for good. Sometimes we cannot imagine how God could possibly be at work in the midst of what seems endlessly wrong. We do not envision the outcomes that God can see, nor do we understand God's time schedule. It can be very frustrating to hope for earthly transformation. Still, the essence of obedience rests in this complete confidence that God has not abandoned us, and is always working for good within as well as beyond the created world.

Take the case of Susan, an independent attorney specializing in corporate law with medium-sized firms. One of her current cases is a legal battle to sever a partnership that has reached an impasse because the judge has declined to proceed until a mutually acceptable agreement is presented. But the bitter feelings between the two former partners are such that both seem willing to let the assets be tied up indefinitely rather than give an inch. Both feel that the other is the one who owes the apology. Subcontractors and employees await long-overdue payments, sometimes with serious economic consequences. Susan wants to believe that God is near and concerned, desiring a beneficial outcome, but she does not know how to proceed. All along she has been praying for both parties in the dispute, but now she feels helpless and a little angry at the childishness of the key players. A breakthrough seems impossible, and Susan suggests to her client and the judge that she be replaced on the case.

However, both urge her to continue, so she figures that for some reason God wants her to work here. If God is the primary "boss," then she must listen in a different way for possible solutions—not within the framework of her client's case, but well beyond. Driving to her office one day, a new idea occurs to Susan. She realizes that in the consistent rejection of reconciliation, both former partners seem strangely alike, bonded to each other in their mutual hatred almost as if it were the two of them against everyone else. What if she were to shift strategies and, instead of seeking out areas of agreement, encourage her client to express all his irrational anger at his former partner and suggest that the opposing attorney do the same? On the surface it seems like a ridiculous idea because there has been far too much name-calling already. But if her hunch is true and the two of them are bound together in a mutual hatred of the justice system, maybe they will join together to resist the "institution's" apparent efforts to alienate them from each other—just as up to now they have resisted the institution's efforts to reconcile them.

After turning over the idea in her mind for some time and not coming up with anything better, Susan sheepishly proposes it to the opposing attorney and the judge. They think it is crazy, too, but they are willing to try anything. When Susan meets with her client privately, she tells him she finally understands his point of view: he has every right to "tar and feather" his former partner. At first he is gratified, but in a few moments he begins to be uneasy and starts arguing with her. Finally he threw her out of his office, shouting that he could malign his old friend but he would be damned if he let anyone else do it! As soon as she left, he called up his former partner and made peace with him. The partnership did terminate, but on a very fair basis for everyone, and the two old partners were golfing buddies again. When it was all over, Susan shook her head and breathed a sign of relief. She had taken a big risk and she wouldn't want to try that strategy very often, but for some strange reason it had worked.

In a certain sense, the impossible task we all share is working with God for transformation. It may seem easier to give up on earth—or to give up on heaven—rather than to hope against hope that they can meet together within our lives. It seems foolish to believe that the divine can work through the creaturely to make a new creation. Yet that is what our faith asks us to believe, not only in the person of Jesus Christ, but also in the ongoing presence of the Holy Spirit in our midst. As St. Paul exclaimed, "Everything has become new! All this is from God, who reconciled us to himself through Christ, and has given us the ministry of reconciliation" (2 Cor. 5:17-18). We have been given the ministry (translated in the Rule as "servanthood") of reconciling the world to God, of allowing God in Christ to work through our lives in the quiet, steady, but never-ending work of bringing all things into their intended glory.

In the soup kitchen or the three-star restaurant, at the construction site or in the boardroom, we are invited to participate in this "impossible task" of reconciliation. Our resources are never enough, but in some mysterious way, our willingness is essential. Obedience is simply this: that we persevere in this work. Whatever the problems, whatever our resources, whatever the horizon, whatever the "results," we work in everything we do as partners with God in the transformation and reconciliation of the world. When we know this, and when it is the focus of every task, then indeed we are both free and powerful in whatever work we do.

Exercises in Obedience

1. Think of a situation in your life in which the external circumstances forced you to stay with something you would have preferred to leave. Explore that experience of the lack of liberty to make a choice, considering specifically what bound you, how you felt about it, and what were the consequences.

Compare that experience with a different situation when you felt stuck not primarily because of outer conditions, but because you were not inwardly free. Circumstances offered options, but you were unable to make a decision, or you did not feel open to a radical new possibility. Again, think about the specific situation, seeking to identify the primary interior cause of your lack of freedom, your feelings, and the consequences.

If you can sense a difference between the experience of lack of liberty and lack of freedom, try to keep that in mind the next time you feel constrained, to help discern which is at work.

2. How do you think a supportive small group of committed Christians could be helpful to you in the integration of your faith and work? If you are not already a member of such a group, consider inviting a few friends to join you to experiment with a few months of meeting to aid mutual discernment and courage.

3. Is there a situation in your life at present, or in the past, that you feel requires your obedience but you are finding difficult? In a time of prayer, bring that situation fully to mind, gently reviewing exactly what is happening and who is involved.

Think about what all the participants are bringing to the situation, and what they hope for as well as what they expect; include yourself in this inventory. As you recreate the situation in your mind, listen very attentively for Christ to help you see something present of which you were previously unaware.

Once you have fully explored all the dimensions of the situation, mentally put the whole thing into an offering plate and lift it up to God, endeavoring to give it all away. Let the burden of responsibility be lifted from your shoulders for now, and rest quietly in God's accepting presence. After a time, mentally ask God how things as they are affect the relationship you have with God. Listen. Then imagine some alternative, and ask God how that change might affect your relationship with God. Sit quietly for a time with what you have heard, remembering to breathe. If you have a new insight, tell it to someone you trust and see how it seems to him or her. If you don't have a new insight, set matters aside, and later return to this process, if you wish.

4. Have you ever experienced feeling fully attuned to another person, such that your thoughts and wills were in perfect harmony, perhaps even acting together without any words being exchanged? If so, reflect on what happened then, and consider whether some elements of it could be called "obedience."

5. In general, do you find yourself resisting suggestions from others, or uncritically accepting whatever you are told? Ponder whether it might be valuable to move a little toward the mean between these two different responses.

6. Think of something which you feel you have earned and have a right to. Write about that thing, how you have worked for it and what it means to you. Then think of something which

you feel is "pure grace," a completely undeserved gift. Write about that, what was given, who gave it, what it means to you. After a time of silently holding the two things together in your heart, explore the connections and dissimilarities between them.

7. Benedict says that there is a "good zeal" and an "evil zeal" (RB 72). Recall a recent time in your work in which you felt what you would call a "good zeal," when you felt passionately and deeply about something in a way that seemed beneficial and right. Then recall another time at work when you experienced more like an "evil zeal," when your passions were high yet you felt there was a destructive or hurtful quality in them. What is the difference in the freedom exercised in both situations? Was there any difference in yourself? If not, reflect on it and talk with others, and see whether you can discover some possibilities. If so, consider what you can do to foster good zeal and minimize evil zeal in yourself.

8. At the present time, in what ways do you regularly serve others? In what ways do others regularly serve you?

9. Read and meditate on the life of the Christian community described in Acts 2 through 5. Compare this with the crises that community faced in Acts 6:1, 11:1-3, 13:44-46, 15:1-21, and 15:36-40. Do any of these conflicts remind you of problems you face in your work setting? How did the Acts community work them through? Do their solutions suggest anything in your situation?

10. With journal in hand, write a page or two completing the following sentence, "If I had infinite time, talent, and treasure, I would...." After you have completed that first segment, read John 1:38, and ponder Jesus' question (to you): "What do

you seek? What are you looking for?" Does that question change anything you have said? If appropriate, add another paragraph to your response.

11. What is your vision of what you would like your workplace to be? What do you now do to prevent it being more like that? What can you choose to do to help move toward that vision?

Conclusion

The Art of Work

Do all for the glory of God.

(RB 57:9)

No discussion of work in the Rule is complete without considering Benedict's chapter 57, called "The Artisans of the Monastery." Over the centuries, one obvious gift of monasticism to the world has been its artistry, its crafts, its love of beauty. One of the most important aspects of human work is its creativity, particularly in that skilled interaction with the created world which makes the heart leap for joy. Monastic artistry has been expressed in music, in sculpture and stained glass, in soaring cathedral arches, in wood and stone.

Benedict expects that those so gifted will express their art in the monastery, and welcomes it as part of the community life. But he insists that balance is necessary here too: crafts are encouraged but not exalted above other contributions to the life of the whole. Work in the kitchen is as important as work on the cathedral, for even artists must be fed. Physical labor is as important as service in the sanctuary, for even garden tools can mediate the divine presence. Benedict is especially aware of the artist's temptation to pride, and is careful to set in place those supports which enable creative work to be sustained over the long term by the artist without an exaggerated sense of self-importance.

Benedict specifies three principles for artisans, which can fruitfully be applied to all human work. The first is having some *vision of one's work as one contribution among many to the whole life of community.* The work of each person is essential to life together. Workers share a common vision of their mutual goal, and have some appreciation of their own part in moving toward that goal. In the Rule, the abbot bears responsibility for conceiving, teaching, and maintaining this common vision, in the context of scripture and the Rule itself. Each worker contributes significantly to the life of the whole, and all prosper when each has a sense of his or her work's value. Similarly, when any worker begins to think too highly of her own contribution, the abbess is to discipline her, even up to removing the worker from that task for a time. Problems arise not when artists (or others) believe they "confer some benefit" on the monastery, but when artists believe their benefit is greater than others. Every worker confers benefit to the whole. But human nature often tends to value some work above others, and this tendency must be corrected by the superior.

Today we might overvalue something other than artistic work. If monetary reward is considered the measure of value, we seem to assign disproportionate importance to sports and entertainment figures and corporate executives. Or perhaps societal value is measured by the amount of media attention or public influence one has. Anyone tempted to conceit on account of his or her work is to take warning, and perhaps withdraw from it for a time until that work can be seen with new perspective. The same remedy applies to anyone tempted to undervalue their work: a perspective-bringing break so they can return to their labor with appreciative eyes!

It is not easy to value ourselves and our work accurately. How do we gain a vision which puts our own work in a perspective that is neither too conceited nor too degrading? In all likelihood, society itself will not give us this vision. We must turn elsewhere—to our religious communities, our churches. Benedict's next two principles for artisans set a framework within which the abbot, or the Christian community, can begin to grow a right vision: do not overcharge or commit fraud in any way, and in all things glorify God.

Do not overcharge or commit fraud. This principle seems almost ridiculous when placed side by side with the sublime principle of glorifying God. Yet Benedict knows them to be somehow equivalent. He reminds us of a chapter in the Acts of the Apostles, which tells of problems that have begun to appear in the community of faith. We remember the story Benedict cites of Ananias and Sapphira:

> If any of the work of the craftsmen is to be sold, let those through whose hands the business has to pass not presume to commit any fraud. Let them remember Ananias and Sapphira (Acts 5:1-11), lest perchance they and all who deal fraudulently with the goods of the monastery should suffer in their souls the death which these incurred in the body. (RB 57:4-6)

Ananias and Sapphira were members of the growing Christian community who lived in the power of the Holy Spirit in the weeks after Pentecost. In gratitude and service, filled with the joy of sharing heart and mind, some people sold excess property and gave the income to the apostles for the care of others. Ananias and Sapphira apparently wanted to be seen as generous, but could not quite bring themselves to give all the receipts from the sale to the community. So they lied, saying they were giving all the proceeds while actually keeping some back for their personal use. But Peter saw through the lie, and both Ananias and Sapphira dropped dead when they were found out.

Benedict's colleague, the Master, interpreted the meaning of this account as showing the danger of dealing in any respect with "worldly affairs," which he felt would inevitably set one's self-will against God's will. He attributed the deaths to the fact that God sees everything. But as usual, Benedict takes a more subtle and less simplistic approach. Ananias and Sapphira were not free in heart and mind. They were pulled in many directions, and instead of being willing to reflect on the many desires that attracted them so that they could establish priorities, they wanted it all. Their wishes were so multifold that they found themselves pretending to be something they were not. And there was no need for the pretense; no one *required* that they sell the land and give the money to the community. The sale was something they *wanted* to do; yet they didn't quite want to do it. They could have chosen to allow their small desire to serve God to grow in them, waiting receptively until they could give simply and wholeheartedly. They could have realized they were not yet ready for such a full commitment, and instead given a little money from time to time. But they did not wait and they acted against love. Benedict understands quite clearly that acting from such constraint causes spiritual death. However small or large the crime against the community, the act of lying, the act of cheating, is a serious crime against oneself and against God. Such fraudulence can occur within or without the monastery, within or without "the world."

Wherever we live, the Christian is called not to overcharge or commit fraud. We can pretend that our actions don't matter, that what we do is invisible, that a little cheating here or a little lying there is not important. Or, we can realize that every action we take, everything we do, every word we speak will either build up something wonderful or drag it down. Each day, in each choice, we are contributing to God's purposes or working against them. Every act moves me toward abundant life, or away from it toward spiritual death. The choice must be made in every moment, and in all the places we find ourselves.

Do all for the glory of God. Many monasteries abbreviate this command over their gates and elsewhere: U.I.O.G.D. *(Ut in omnibus glorificetur Deus).* What can it mean? It must mean at least behaving honorably. But at best perhaps it also means obedience to God in the fullest sense of the term: acting in full freedom toward the One whom we love without measure. Glorifying God includes vocation, being who we are, as well as stewardship, care for what is given us. Certainly it means acknowledging our dependence upon God in obedience. But there is something more here, the final secret to the integration of work and faith. And that is the gift of the altar: the consecration of our work.

I consecrate my work by giving it to God, by being obedient to God in everything and offering all to God. Whatever I do, I do it for the love of God, as best I can, in confidence that God is pleased to receive my efforts. Benedict is echoing 1 Peter in his phrase, "that in all God may be glorified":

> Above all, maintain constant love for one another, for love covers a multitude of sins. Be hospitable to one another without complaining. Like good stewards of the manifold grace of God, serve one another with whatever gift each of you has received. Whoever speaks must do so as one speaking the very words of God; whoever serves must do so with the strength that God supplies, so that God may be glorified in all things through Jesus Christ. (1 Peter 4:8-11, partially cited in RB 57:9)

We are stewards not only of our own talents, but also of the "manifold grace of God." God's very life is somehow made visible within creation when we work in love of God. Do I sometimes experience my work as a distraction from God? Let me then look again, realizing that when I am really present to my work, I am present to God, who is the sustaining mystery of all.

1 Peter continues with a reminder that sometimes we experience our work as a fiery ordeal, as a test of faith, as suffering. No matter. Let us then entrust ourselves to God, as Jesus did, continuing to do good. There will be hard, if not impossible, tasks thrust upon us, and there are many times when we will experience a darkness of knowing and a doubt of faith. But in all, let us simply hand it over to God. Whatever is happening, within and without, we offer it to God. When work feels empty, wrong, inadequate, or difficult, we do as well as we can, and offer it to God. It is the simple act of offering what we have to God that consecrates it. We give our life to God's hands, where it is made holy:

> By hard work, live the daily Passover from suffering to offering, from constraint to acceptance; and from merely being submissive, you will become a son sharing the Father's work. Thus unified, may you do all for God's glory.[1]

Every life has its demands and frustrations; every life has its limits. Every employment has its constraints that can be opportunities for offering our work wholly to God. We can give to God what we do not understand, and receive it back enfolded in God's very life. In this way, our obedience becomes a tool in support of God's ongoing work in the world. For God actively desires our collaboration in the continuing creation of the world, and we are invited to see our daily work as a sacred contribution to God's work itself.

Nothing Harsh, Nothing Burdensome

We have offered three central perspectives in this book, drawn from the Rule of St. Benedict, whose purpose is to help all Christians more fully experience the unity of work and faith. Vocation: know yourself called by God and someone essential to God's purpose. Stewardship: receive the situation of your life as gift, and care for it with reverence. Obedience: seek God in everything, to serve and be served in freedom.

Will such work change the world? If we labor in accordance with vocation, stewardship, and obedience, can our lives make a difference? Does sacred work make a sacred society? The answer to these questions is ambiguous. Maybe our work will effect change in the organizations we serve, and maybe not. Maybe there will be a noticeable impact because of our fidelity to God, and maybe not. Maybe the sacred work of a growing number of Christians will be the leaven gradually to permeate the whole cultural context of our time, and maybe not. Benedict's life suggests to us that the answers to such questions do not matter. The institutions of our time may continue to decay and may eventually collapse; our churches may continue to be mostly lukewarm, our corporations may continue to be mostly greedy, and our bureaus may continue to be mostly ineffectual.

It does not matter whether the institutions are salvageable or not because, in the long run, their dissolution may be what is required to allow entry of the fresh new life of the Spirit. The Roman civilization of Benedict's time had seemed to be an essential source of stability for many centuries, and yet it was already well on its way to disintegration. God can be served at all times in history, and in many ways other than contributing to progress. Benedict and Scholastica chose to serve God. They joined in community with others who likewise yearned to serve God. They prayed together and lived a simple but not spartan life. They welcomed the poor and the hungry, the stranger and the sinner. Books were studied and laboriously copied; beauty was created and enjoyed; God was thanked and praised. At first it seemed that their lives contributed very little to the grand scheme of things, and for several hundred years the Rule was little known and seldom used. It seemed to disappear from European history until the early ninth century, when Charlemagne prescribed its use in all the monasteries of his Holy Roman Empire.

If working according to the principles of vocation and stewardship and obedience will not change the world, then will we at least find happiness as individuals? At least let us be assured that if we take on this strenuous labor of holy work, we will be wealthy and healthy and wise. Maybe we cannot solve the world's problems, but at least let us solve our own! If we take up the challenge of sacred work, will we find relief from the stresses that plague us?

Again the answer is—perhaps. There can be no certainty that a life responding to call, taking care, and serving one another will be easier than not doing those things. As we have seen, working according to these principles may actually create more tension in our lives, at least for a time. If our work is a challenge to the status quo, being obedient in our vocation may evoke hostility, even if undertaken lovingly. Inner anxieties may increase, and the way ahead may seem obscure. As Jesus' life so clearly demonstrates, the service of God is seldom easy.

Benedict warns that the way is bound to be narrow at times but he also insists that it is not meant to be harsh or burdensome (RB Prologue 46, 48). We can be certain that when our whole desire is attuned to the love of God, and when we apply that desire concretely to the daily tasks before us, God will be at work in us and with us. Though we may never know what exterior impact the service of God produces, we can be assured that our very desire to seek God emerges as response to God's prior seeking of us. God wants our salvation and yearns to bring the whole world to its intended fullness in

Christ. When we endeavor to cooperate with God in this work, we know that we are being changed from glory to glory, whether we sense it or not. Somehow and sometime, the intended fruit will ripen, whether we see it or not. This is indeed work as the friend of our soul.

Throughout this book the imagery of Isaiah has appeared as a symbol of the way God is at work in our work.

For as the rain and the snow come down from heaven, and do not return there until they have watered the earth, making it bring forth and sprout, giving seed to the sower and bread to the eater, so shall my word be that goes out from my mouth; it shall not return to me empty, but it shall accomplish that which I purpose, and succeed in the thing for which I sent it. (Isa. 55:10-11)

Human work is soul-befriending when it is in unity with this fruitful essence of God. We are sent from God, just as the rain and snow are sent to water the earth. When we do our part, God assures that there will be seed and bread enough—for us, and for all. Let us with gladness take up this work together.

Endnotes

Introduction
1. See Vatican II's *Gaudium et Spes,* the Pastoral Constitution on the Church in the Modern World, ed. Abbott-Gallagher, p. 67, for a similar statement of vision about human work.

Chapter One: In Times Like These
1. For elaboration of this perspective, see William Carroll Bark, *Origins of the Medieval World* (New York: Doubleday Anchor, 1960). For example, Bark notes:

> We know now that the Dark Age was not all that dark.... Medieval society was functional in ways not even dreamed of by antiquity.... It was a working, striving society, impelled to pioneer, forced to experiment, often making mistakes but also drawing upon the energies of its people much more fully than its predecessors, and eventually allowing them much fuller and freer scope for development. (p. 98)

> The beginning of the Middle Ages was a pioneering movement.... Frontiers need not always be geographical, and the relationship of the old to the new is not invariably, as in more recent times, that of a vigorous, relatively rich, technically much superior culture to one numerically weak, economically poor, and technically backward. Nonetheless, there were wildernesses and savages to

contend with and a new way of life to create.... The molders and bearers of the rising society were the monasteries. (pp. 107-108)

2. Josef Pieper, *Scholasticism* (London: 1961), p. 16.

Chapter Two: Vocation

1. Dorothy Sayers, "Living to Work," originally a radio broadcast, reprinted in *Unpopular Opinions* (London: Victor Gollancz Ltd., 1946), p. 122.

2. C. S. Lewis, ed., *George MacDonald: 365 Readings* (New York: Collier Books/Macmillan, 1947), pp. 7-10. Lewis has collected excerpts of his favorite reflections from MacDonald's work.

3. Frederick Buechner, *Wishful Thinking: A Theological ABC* (New York: Harper and Row, 1973), p. 95.

4. Studs Terkel, *Working: People Talk About What They Do All Day and How They Feel About What They Do* (New York: Pantheon Books, 1972), p. xi.

5. *Time* (December 19, 1994), p. 75.

6. *America's 50 Fastest Growing Jobs,* compiled by J. Michael Farr (Indianapolis: JIST Works Inc., 1995), p. 1.

7. "The 1992—2005 Job Outlook in Brief," in *Occupational Outlook Quarterly* of the U. S. Department of Labor, Bureau of Labor Statistics (vol. 38: no. 1/Spring 1994), p. 7.

8. I am grateful to my neighbor, Dr. Anne Dunlea, a linguist and occupational therapist at the University of Southern California, for these categories.

9. Although he uses the concept in a slightly different way, I am indebted to Martin Cawley, OSCO, for the concept of the "abbot as a connoisseur of the artworks which are the lives of his monks." See "Four Themes in the Rule of Saint Benedict," *Word and Spirit: A Monastic Review* (Still River, Mass: St. Bede's Publications, 1981),vol. 2, p. 109.

10. Pelagius was a Christian priest-monk in Britain who insisted that the fullness of Christian life was meant for every Christian. He then went on to argue that perfection could be achieved by humans merely through the beneficial exercise of their own wills, for which he was declared a heretic. He was a contemporary of St. Augustine of Hippo in the fifth century, and evoked some of Augustine's best-known writings.

11. Emily Dickinson, *Final Harvest*, selection by T. H. Johnson (Boston: Little, Brown and Co., 1961), p. 248. This section of the poem reads:

Tell all the Truth but tell it slant—
Success in Circuit lies
Too bright for our infirm Delight
The Truth's superb surprise.

12. For more insight into these "disciplines" of listening, responding, and being transformed, see my earlier book in this series, *No Moment Too Small,* which discusses at length how to integrate these Benedictine elements into life in the world.

13. Buechner, *Wishful Thinking,* p. 95.

14. From a speech by the Right Reverend George Carey, Archbishop of Canterbury, in Washington, D.C., on September 11, 1992, sponsored by Trinity Church, Wall Street, New York City.

Chapter Three: Stewardship

1. Fredrica Harris Thompsett, *Courageous Incarnation: In Intimacy, Work, Childhood, and Aging* (Cambridge, Mass.: Cowley Publications, 1993), p. 107.

2. Bill Fenley, vice-president of sales and marketing at Cache Computers in Fremont, quoted in a *Los Angeles Times* article titled "Feeling Tense? You're Probably Doing Your Job" (April 29, 1990), p. 1.

3. Thomas Merton, *Conjectures of a Guilty Bystander* (Garden City, N. Y.: Image Doubleday, 1968), p. 68.

4. The idea of stewardship as doing ordinary things "tenderly and competently" comes from Esther de Waal's *Seeking God* (Collegeville, Minn.: The Liturgical Press, 1984), p. 106, where she gives credit to Jean Vanier, *Community and Growth* (London: Darton, Longman, and Todd, 1979), p. 220. Robert Bellah used similar language when he talked about "careful power" in the workplace during a sermon given at the Preaching Excellence '91 Conference at the Church Divinity School of the Pacific, June 4, 1991, and printed in *Sermons that Work* (Cincinnati: Forward Movement Publications, 1991), p. 76.

5. Cardinal Basil Hume, *Searching for God* (London: Hodder and Stoughton, 1977), p. 73.

6. *The Rule of the Master,* trans. Luke Eberle, OSB (Kalamazoo: Cistercian Publications, 1977), Chapter 86, p. 251. *(Italics mine.)*

7. Adalbert de Vogue, *The Rule of Saint Benedict: A Doctrinal and Spiritual Commentary,* trans. John Baptist Hasbrouck (Kalamazoo: Cistercian Publications, 1983), p. 241.

8. Daniel Rees, *et al, Consider Your Call: A Theology of Monastic Life Today* (Kalamazoo: Cistercian Publications, 1978), p. 43.

9. Quoted by Robert Bellah in a speech on "Discipleship and Citizenship in the Workplace" offered at Fuller Theological Seminary, March 1990.

10. I am indebted for this idea to Michael Paternoster, *Counsels for All Christians: Obedience, Stability and Conversion in the Rule of St. Benedict* (Oxford: SLG Press, 1980), p. 4: "Our age is in some respects not materialistic enough, we have insufficient respect for things in themselves."

Chapter Four: Obedience

1. Harold J. Laski, *Liberty in the Modern State* (New York: The Viking Press, 1949), p. 172.

2. See Robert N. Bellah, Richard Madsen, William M. Sullivan, Ann Swidler, and Steve M. Tipton, *The Good Society* (New York: Random House/Vintage Books, 1992).

3. Augustine of Hippo, *The City of God,* Book XIV. See also *The Enchiridion on Faith, Hope, and Love,* chapter 30, and Augustine's arguments against Pelagius. A particularly good discussion of Augustine's life-long preoccupation with the meaning of human freedom appears in Peter Brown's biography of Augustine, *Augustine of Hippo* (New York: Dorset Press, 1967).

4. Martin Buber, *Between Man and Man* (New York: Macmillan, 1965), p. 91.

5. Esther de Waal, *A Life-Giving Way* (London: Geoffrey Chapman, 1995), p. 41.

6. *The Rule of the Master,* trans. Luke Eberle (Kalamazoo: Cistercian Publications, 1977), chapter VII: verse 55, p. 123.

Chapter Five: The Art of Work

1. Pierre-Marie Delfieux, *The Jerusalem Community Rule of Life* (Mahweh, N.J.: Paulist Press, 1985), p. 18. The Jerusalem Fraternities were founded in urban Paris in the 1970s, inspired by the way of life of the Little Brothers and Sisters of Jesus.

Suggestions for Further Reading

Integrating work and spirit in general

Robert Bellah, Richard Madsen, William Sullivan, Ann Swidler, and Steve Tipton, *The Good Society* (New York: Vintage Books, 1992).

William Diehl, *The Monday Connection* (San Francisco: Harper Collins, 1991).

Matthew Fox, *The Reinvention of Work: A New Vision of Livelihood for our Time* (San Francisco: Harper, 1994). See especially the helpful questionnaire on pages 309f.

Vaclev Havel, *Living in Truth* (Boston: Faber & Faber, 1989).

Parker Palmer, *The Active Life: Wisdom for Work, Creativity, and Caring* (San Francisco: Harper, 1991).

Dorothy Soelle and Shirley Cloyes, *To Work and To Love* (Philadelphia: Fortress Press, 1984).

Fredrica Harris Thompsett, *Courageous Incarnation: In Intimacy, Work, Childhood, and Aging* (Cambridge, Mass.: Cowley Publications, 1993).

Douglas C. Vest, *Why Stress Keeps Returning: A Spiritual Response* (Chicago: Loyola University Press, 1991).

Claude Whitmyer, ed., *Mindfulness and Meaningful Work: Explorations in Right Livelihood* (Berkeley: Parallax Press, 1994). Compare the Buddhist approach of this book with the Christian and Benedictine tradition.

Monastic work and faith

Charles Cummings, OSCO, *Monastic Practices* (Kalamazoo: Cistercian Publications, 1986).

Pierre-Marie Delfieux, *The Jerusalem Community Rule of Life* (Mahweh, N. J.: Paulist Press, 1985).

Esther de Waal, *Seeking God: The Way of St. Benedict* (Collegeville, Minn.: The Liturgical Press, 1980).

Esther de Waal, *A Life-Giving Way* (London: Geoffrey Chapman, 1995).

Daniel Rees, *et al, Consider Your Call: A Theology of Monastic Life Today* (Kalamazoo: Cistercian Publications, 1980).

Cowley Publications is a ministry of the Society of St. John the Evangelist, a religious community for men in the Episcopal Church. Emerging from the Society's tradition of prayer, theological reflection, and diversity of mission, the press is centered in the rich heritage of the Anglican Communion.

Cowley Publications seeks to provide books, audio cassettes, and other resources for the ongoing theological exploration and spiritual development of the Episcopal Church and others in the body of Christ. To this end, it is dedicated to developing a new generation of theological writers, encouraging them to produce timely, creative, and stimulating publications of excellence, and making these publications available widely, reaching both clergy and lay persons.